GLOBALISATION *or* RECOLONISATION ?

The Muslim World in the ***21st Century***

G000060290

Ali Mohammadi & Muhammad Ahsan

Ta-Ha Publishers Ltd.
London

Published in 2002

by

Ta-Ha Publishers Ltd.
1 Wynne Road
London SW9 0BB
Website: http//www.taha.co.uk
e-mail: sales@taha.co.uk

A catalogue records of this book is available from the
British Library cataloguing in Publication Data
Mohammadi, Ali
Muslim world in the 21st century : globalisation or recolonisation?
1.   Islam – 20th century 2. Islamic countries – Civilization
I. Title II. Muhammad, Ahsan
909'. 0917671

ISBN 1 84200 032 2

Printed in England by De-Luxe Printers
London NW10 7NR
e-mail: de-luxe@talk21.com

Dedicated to the rulers of the Muslim World who cannot see the writings on the wall

Contents

List of Tables

Abbreviations

ABM	Anti- Ballistic Missile
ACM	Arab Common Market
AFTA	Arab Free Trade area
AMU	Arab Maghreb Union
ASEAN	Association of South East Asian Countries
BCCI	Bank of Credit and Commerce International
CACEU	Central African Customs and Economic Union
CAR	Central African Republics
CTBT	Comprehensive Test Ban Treaty
D-8	Developing Eight
ECO	Economic Cooperation Organisation
EU	European Union
FAS	Federation of American Scientists
FMA	Foreign Military Assistance
FMF	Foreign Military Financing
GATT	General Agreement of Tariff and Trade
GCC	Gulf Cooperation Council
GDP	Gross Domestic Product
GNP	Gross National Product
HDF	Human Development Fund
HDI	Human Development Index
HIPC	Highly Indebted Poor Countries
ICCI&CE	Islamic Chambers of Commerce, Industry and Commodity Exchange
ICDT	Islamic Centre for the Development of Trade
IDB	Islamic Development Bank
IDF	Islamic Defence Force

IEU	Islamic Economic Union
IFSTD	Islamic Foundation for Science, Technology and Development
IINA	International Islamic News Agency
IISS	International Institute for Strategic Studies
IMF	International Monitory Fund
ISBO	Islamic States Broadcasting Organisation
ISC	Islamic Security Council
ITO	International Trade Organisation
MMF	Muslim Monitory Fund
MFN	Most Favoured Nation
NAFTA	North American Free Trade Agreement
NATO	North Atlantic Treaty Organisation
NPT	Non-Proliferation Treaty
OIC	Organisation of Islamic Conference
PPP	Purchasing Power Parities
SAP	Structural Adjustment Programme
TNC	Trans-national Corporations
UNCTAD	United Nations Conference on Trade and Development
UNDP	United Nations Development Programme
WAEC	West African Economic Community
WTO	World Trade Organisation

Preface

Globalisation is not merely an economic phenomenon but concerns human values. Although there is a minority, if admitted vigorous, anti-globalisation movement in the West, mainly from the radical left and some environmentalists, there is a general acceptance of the premises on which globalisation is based. This is largely because the stress on material goods and consumerism accords with the motivating force of Western secularist societies. For Muslims, however, globalisation presents a challenge to their basic beliefs. A hierarchy of peoples and nations based on material wealth that leaves the Islamic World marginalised at the bottom of the pecking order may be uncontroversial in the West, but it is certainly challenged by thinking Muslims.

Ali Mohammadi and Muhammad Ahsan address these crucial issues highlighting the economic injustices for the Muslim World arising from the present and evolving global order. Central to this is the issue of indebtedness; with the paradox that despite the condemnation of interest based financing in the Quran. Governments in the Muslim World have relied heavily on such funding. Muslim countries are also becoming ever more exploited in their trade relations, as the WTO agenda forces them into becoming suppliers of low labour cost goods and potentially scarce resources, while at the same time overpaying for western goods and services because of a distorted global pricing system.

The Western media likes to depict Islamic fundamentalism as a threat, while not acknowledging the threat of their own civilisation to others. The authors turns this on its head by identifying Western fundamentalism as the threat, citing as evidence the cases of Palestine, Iraq, Sudan, Somalia, Kashmir and East Timor where western intervention has been disastrous for Muslim interests. Muslim countries are portrayed as aggressive and militaristic by some sections of the western media. Yet defence spending per capita, per soldiers and the proportion of population employed in the armed services is much lower for Muslim countries than for Non-Muslim states, even when allowances are made for disparities in income levels.

How should the Muslim World confront these global injustices? Mohammadi and Ahsan urge greater Muslim solidarity and unity, building on institutions that are already established such as the Organisation of Islamic Conference, the Islamic Development Bank, the International Islamic News Agency and, Islamic Foundation for Science, Technology and Development. They both see the need to promote trade between Muslim countries, and encourage the integration of regional capital markets rather than simply tolerating capital flight to the West. The rulers of the Muslim World will have to wake up, however, if any of these recommendations are to become a reality.

Professor Rodney Wilson
Centre for Middle Eastern and Islamic Studies
University of Durham

Introduction

Today's world is changing with such incredible pace and speed that the present international and national systems are finding it increasingly difficult to accommodate and adapt to the new shifting environments. The eleventh of September 2001 terrorist attacks on the World Trade Centre in New York city, was not only an attack on a nation but also on one of the leading symbols of global capitalism. The attacks clearly indicate that despite the seemingly unstoppable march of corporate global capitalism, life, for the present, and the foreseeable future, in the North has become uncertain and insecure. Similarly, the terrorist attack on the Pentagon, the symbolic representation of US military power, was taken by many to be a militant and angry response to US military and foreign policy interference and exploitation of many countries in the South. The lack of concern by the rich Northern powers in eradicating the injustice and impoverishment that is a daily fact of life for the majority of the world's population leads to feelings of dispossession, discontent and resentment. This resentment has often boiled over into anger and violent militant action that can act as a destabilising factor in world affairs, even in the heartland of the only existing military super power, and as a result, against which most of this anger is directed, the United States.

One way to analyse these suicide attacks is to place them within the context of many years of US biased foreign policy and direct influence in the internal affairs of many countries in the South. In this situation, the question of global insecurity has become an important issue of the globalised world. This has manifested itself in the social, economic and political arena. In fact, to this development can be attributed many positive aspects, many of which have contributed, and continue to contribute to, the rapidly developing global system as a whole. During the nineteenth century, and in the first half of the twentieth century, scientific development benefited all of mankind in more or less equal terms. Inventions such as the aeroplane, motorcycle, railway, buses, cars, telephone, refrigerator, radio, television, vaccines, antibiotics, vitamins, electricity and many other things, helped to bridge the gap between the working classes and the elite. Prices were deliberately kept low to enable everyone to avail of these new inventions. The trend, however, was to change after the Second World War. Today, the direction of this development is prefixed only by the pursuit of profit and greed. These modern developments are taking the place of the factory and office worker, and replacing worker with robotic machines and computers that are quicker and cheaper.

It is over a period of two decades that we are studying and researching the process and the impact of globalisation in the world today. Some scholars are excited and positive about what they perceive to be the benefits of globalisation while others take a more sceptical and critical view of the process. An issue of prime importance within these approaches is to examine how Muslims scholars' view the globalisation process and how the process itself has effected and impinged upon the developing world in general and the Muslim World in particular. In order to find out the Islamist responses to the globalisation process and its impact on the Muslim countries; we need to examine the state of Muslim countries in relation to the Non-Muslim World and evaluate how the Muslim World is reacting to the process of globalisation. First, it is crucial to find out how the Islamic scholars have reacted to the globalisation process. Ali Mazrui (1998) an Islamist critic carefully looks at globalisation from the viewpoint of power within an historical context; he places the basis of his analysis on four main forces: religion, technology, economy, and the role of empire. He suggests that the combination of all these four categories have created a globalisation process, which he sees as ultimately leading to a homogenised as well as a culturally hegemonised world. He argues that the outcome of globalisation has been homogenisation with a disproportionate share of power in the hands of a few countries which have total control of the hegemonic centre. He sees the cause of all this change as emanating from the liberation of the market economy as enforced by the International Monetary Fund (IMF) and the World Bank. The expansion of a Euro-centric culture based on the market economy has produced an unjust and imbalanced global culture and economy to the extent that, according to the World Bank's President, over 1.7 billion people are currently living in extreme poverty (World Bank, 1999).

What Mazrui is trying to say from an economic point of view is nothing new, Samir Amin (1997) has said much the same thing, and in a clearer way. For him, the inequalities of the present global system is, in fact, the outcome of the unequal development of capitalism and the consolidation, and continuation of five monopolies. Firstly, the technological monopoly, he argues, is in the hands of a few wealthy western nations which can afford to spend enormous amounts of money on military research and technologies of mass destruction. Secondly, the determining factor of finance in the stock markets of New York, London, Frankfurt and Tokyo, which control the global market. Thirdly, global elite has created a system of monopolistic access and strict control of the planet's natural resources. At present capitalism is not concerned with questions of ecology – exploitation and short-term profit are the primary goals. Fourthly, the major component of the market economy and global capitalism is media and communication monopolies. The fifth and final monopoly in Samir Amin's view is the monopoly over weapons of mass destruction. He believes that the foundation of globalisation is based on these five monopolies. However, he fails to see, like Mazrui, the extraordinary innovations that communication technologies have provided in the last three decades in facilitating this rapid global shift and transformation of the world economy.

For past few centuries, the international trade has been dominating in the world's politico-economic affairs. However, in this context what has emerged with such magnitude in the last two decades is the deterioration of the technological application and cultural dimension of the world economy, which in turn has caused the destabilisation of nation-states. In the Muslim World, Indonesia is a case in point. Amin (1997) in this context concludes that the 'accumulation of all these transformations has resulted in the collapse of the equilibrium of the post-war world system. Mazrui further elaborates on the force of technology and suggests that globalisation was the outcome of the final stage in history, the marriage of industrial revolution with information technology, with the end result to be found between homogenisation and hegemonisation.

Homogenisation is clearly the result of democratic access to the market. As access to the market becomes easier and more apparent we will eventually become more alike as a result of similar consumption patterns. However, what is important to note here is the question of hegemonisation. The globalisation process began not too long ago, with the participation of the seven industrial nations known as G-7. What has since emerged is the fact that the cultural dimension of economic globalisation has become its most powerful attribute. This has manifested itself in the unhindered expansion and spread of western culture in general and corporate America in particular.

As the market economy and market liberalisation are gradually expanding through access to other cultures being encroached upon as the market expands, hegemonisation may shift, or at least balance itself out. This occurs as a result of the emerging culture gaining more access to computer technology and the internet giving them the ability to compete and participate in the global market. Thus, access to the internet is increasing the proliferation of culture and information technology, transforming them into a new commodity which is very vital to the survival and perpetuation of the globalised economy. Today, the main developments that have occurred in the West are as a consequence of modernity, which in itself is the result of scientific research and rationality. The Western world, since the time of the Crusades, has realised that progress in research and development is the only means by which humankind can develop and progress.

It is noteworthy that a French general, after the Treaty of Versailles and the dismemberment of the Ottoman Empire entered the Umayyad mosque, in which lays the body of Saladin (a Muslim hero famous for his victories over the crusaders), and kicking the tomb cried, 'Saladin, wake up, we are back' (Latouch, 1996). The Muslim World for its part failed to engage in a critical debate in order to attempt to understand and comprehend the reasons as to why they had fallen behind the West in terms of progress and development. What needs to be recognised is the fact that if they fail to do so they will be unable to compete in the present globalised world and this gap will inevitably widen. In trying to find an answer to the underdevelopment of Muslim countries, and to explain why they have failed to learn from the bitter historical experiences of colonisation and economic stagnation, we must critically examine the causes and their influence on these countries status in the current globalised world before suggesting possible remedies and solutions for the ills of the Muslim World as a whole. This is the undertaking of the book.

The first chapter focuses on globalisation in theory and action. It evaluates the state of the Muslim World in the context of globalisation and the prospect for success in the struggle of an unequal race at the dawn of the twenty-first century. The second chapter examines the major differences between the developed and the developing worlds in relation to the globalisation process. It explores the contemporary state of the Muslim World with regard to development and discusses the way in which Islam as a religion is portrayed in the West. This chapter also looks at the foreign powers and the way they have influenced the Muslim World and how the lack of solidarity and sympathetic leadership have failed to unite the Muslim countries towards a system of mutual cooperation.

The third chapter looks at the current global financial system and its impact on the Third World countries, particularly the question of debt burden. This chapter focuses on the globalisation of the debt trap and its impact on Muslim countries and argues that debt relief for a number of countries could enable them to use these funds for investment. Chapter four carefully explores the gap in the trade trap and the increasing hopes among nations following the end of super power confrontation. It also examines the prospects of the Islamic economic market. Chapter five discusses the implications of defence and development in the age of globalisation. Today, the United States is the biggest producer and largest exporter of arms to other countries. This chapter also provides a comparison of defence expenditure between Muslim and Non-Muslim countries. It is interesting to note that Muslim countries import less arms than other Non-Muslim countries, but still spend approximately US$ 70 billion a year.

The sixth chapter provides a critical analysis of Western fundamentalism in the context of present global politics and focuses on a few case studies of international problems in relation to the Muslim World in conjunction with examining the role of the major players and their allies. Chapter seven of the book evaluates the contemporary situation of information technology and global media as a proxy for another Cold War and examines the role of those corporations which inform and diffuse news. It also highlights the need for major media corporations belong to Muslim countries.

The final chapter explores the possible ways and means with which to improve the overall states of development in the Muslim World. It also sets out to consider and examine the widespread causes of poverty, illiteracy and deprivation that continue to exist in the Muslim World. This is a particularly pertinent point for the development of these countries, and global development as a whole, given the fact that at present Muslims comprise almost a quarter of the world's total population. This chapter presents a comprehensive future strategy for the Muslim World.

The authors hope that this text can contribute to a further understanding of the present state of Muslim countries, particularly with regard to the cause and effect of under-development and the lack of unity amongst the Muslim leaders. The indicative case studies provide a clear picture of the current problems that beset the Muslim World in the age of rapid globalisation.

1

Globalisation - Theory and Practice

What is globalisation?

Globalisation is the outcome of deregulation in the economic market and the integration of information technology in trade, banking, broadcast media and telecommunications. This worldwide phenomenon 'is a coalescence of various transnational processes and domestic structures, allowing the economy, politics, culture, and ideology of one country to penetrate another. The chain of causality runs from the spatial reorganisation of production to international trade and to the integration of financial markets. This is a market-induced, not a policy led, process (Mittelman, 1997:3). In fact, in every sphere of life, the twentieth century has brought rapid changes to the world, especially the present globalisation process involved in the geographical extension of economic activities in general and the functional integration of internationally dispersed activities in particular (Dicken, 1998:5). Consequently, the degree of interdependence and interconnection within the world economy has increased dramatically. So far, 'the process of globalisation has produced much that is new in the world's economy and politics, but it has not changed the basic ways in which capitalism operates. Furthermore, it has done little to aid the cause of either peace or prosperity' (Magdoff, 1992:41).

One of the main problems for developing countries in general, and Muslim countries in particular, is how to integrate these changes into their own political, economic and cultural systems. This problem is particularly acute given the fact that many developing nations lack the basic infrastructure needed in order to receive the benefits of globalisation. If the process of change is not smoothly integrated into existing systems it can disrupt the whole process of a country's development, leading to political instability, social and religious tensions, and economic imbalances. Indonesia is a case in point. As a part of the rapidly growing global economy it has consistently failed to achieve or implement the World Bank and IMF prescribed economic targets and measures, and as a result the entire structure of the Indonesian economy has collapsed.

Without an examination of the actual functions of the IMF and the World Bank, especially those that have occurred since the 1980s, defining the globalisation process and its impact becomes almost impossible. This arises from the fact that these two leading international financial institutions have played a crucial role in the whole process of the global transformation of capital. Such a situation has become particularly acute since the collapse of Soviet bloc, given the latter's position as the main rival ideological force in the international political economy. The conservative forces in North America and Western Europe have prepared public opinion for this transformation by controlling large sections of the mass media conglomerates, which in turn have actively pushed forward the idea of market deregulation in order to achieve the free flow of capital and the removal of government limitations to the expansion of global finance. Furthermore, the globalisation process has been implemented, strengthened and promoted through the support mechanism of international financial institutions such as the World Bank and the IMF (Mohammadi, 1997).

This chapter can be considered as a self-reflective narrative and a personal dialogue in the context of the globalisation paradigm. After receiving positive responses to the book entitled *Globalisation and International Communication* (Mohammadi, 1997), the present book attempts to analyse the situation of the contemporary world at the end of the second millennium and to evaluate the position of the Muslim World as a case study in the context of the globalisation process. In other words, where does the Muslim World stand on the globalisation highway, and what are the future prospects for the world if this trend remains as it is today?

Due to the integration of the world, Marshall McLuhan (1964) has suggested that, 'Man now lives in a global-sized village, and is returning to the values and perceptions of a preliterate culture.' At the dawn of the third millennium we are actually experiencing a situation where peoples and their cultures are exhibiting increasingly hybrid characteristics. Although, it can be argued that much of this is not new, as human beings have always been engaged in a process of interaction throughout history, today's 'globalisation' is different, primarily because of the speed with which it is taking place. It is driven by new forms of connectivity, such as the internet, and is governed by different rules, or, in many cases, by no rules at all. At present we are unable to assess the impact of instant communication across national borders or its effect on culture, politics, economy, finance, ecology and human socio-psychological environment. This is due to the fact that the history of this phenomenon is not of substantial length to be able to accurately measure its impact on mankind. However, one factor has emerged that holds significant repercussions for us all, and that is the fact that, the rapid changes which have occurred in the last decade of twentieth century have all arisen as a result of the modernisation process and its consequent destabilisation effects. As Hobsbawm (1999) suggested, 'globalisation means wider, but not necessarily equal, access for all and will lead to an increase in disparity between the 'haves and have nots'. Globalisation provides people with more choices and creates new opportunities for prosperity, as well as making people more familiar and aware of global diversity. However, millions of people around the world experience globalisation not as an agent of progress, or as Giddens (1998) suggests 'a consequence of modernity', but as a disruptive force, almost hurricane-like in its ability to destroy lives, jobs and traditions. For many there is an urge to resist the process and take refuge in the illusory comforts of nationalism, fundamentalism or other such 'isms'. As a result of the rapidly growing market, huge potential benefits are on offer for some, whilst at the same time incredible perils befall many nations of the developing world.

These developments are very similar to the situation that gave rise to the division of the world into Westernisation versus colonisation, however, with one significant difference, through decolonisation, the architects of the westernisation process eventually discovered their wrongdoings. Now, as Latouche (1996: 6) suggests, 'the white man has gone offstage, while science, technology and development have taken over.' In fact, the changes in the global economy over the past three decades have seen the emergence of a new phase of capitalism that has lead to the globalisation of markets, trade and labour (Offe, 1985; Lipietz, 1987; Lash & Urry, 1997; Featherstone, 1992). Therefore, globalisation as a concept refers both to the compression of the world as well as its intensification (Robertson, 1992). Giddens (1998) argues that 'the development of the sovereignty of the modern state from its beginnings depends upon a reflexively monitored set of relations between states.' In this context, globalisation, is a process of historical change and in modern times is defined, by Robertson, (1987) as 'the crystallization of the entire world as a single place,' resulting in the emergence of a global-human condition.

As mentioned above, globalisation is not a new phenomenon but what is new is the extent and pace at which global integration has taken place, particularly during the last two decades. This trend has been most evident in the post-war era, but can be seen to have existed even before that in the early period of the twentieth century. The process of globalisation has accelerated with the restructuring of the global capital economy but the present struggle can be understood as a resumption of previous trends that, ended abruptly with the first world war and the great depression. The creation of the General Agreement on Tariff and Trade (GATT), in the early post-war period, was an institutional attempt (Bannock and Etal, 1992: 179-180) to begin negotiations aimed at lowering tariff and trade barriers. This institution was eventually replaced by the World Trade Organisation (WTO) in 1995, which continued to operate with the same remit. In this context, globalisation has restructured the role of the state, which has become merely a vehicle for transmitting global market discipline onto the domestic economy. It has given increased power to capital investors, multinational firms and global financial institutions. These actors dictate their own terms to states and, if not adhered to, many retaliate by either speculating against the country in world currency markets, as disclosed by recent East Asian currency crises, or fuelling political instability and social unrest leading to the removal of governments. President Suharto in Indonesia provides a good example of a ruler ousted from power by the pressure exerted from these actors.

In addition, the imposed privatisation and deregulation policies that are pursued through structural adjustment programmes under the dictates of IMF and the World Bank have led to socio-political destabilisation in many countries. Consequently, states are unable to deliver on the promises and expectations of the masses because they have lost control over their national economies. In the absence of domestic cultural economic cohesion, the forces of internal disintegration intensify, thus threatening the very existence of the state itself. This discussion reflects the fact that globalisation has many dimensions, in much the same way as different people have different opinions. Sachs (2000: 113), a modern Western thinker, argues that 'today's world is divided not by ideology but by technology. ... With the end of the cold war, old ideological divisions are over. Virtually all nations proclaim allegiance to a global market, but an intractable division is taking hold, this time based on technology. A small part of the globe, accounting for some 15% of the earth's population, provides nearly all of the world's technology innovations. A second part, involving perhaps half of the world's population is able to adopt these technologies in production and consumption. The remaining part, covering around a third of the world's population, is technologically disconnected, neither innovating at home nor adopting foreign technologies.'

A careful consideration of Sachs declaration reflects that he is only partially right in his assumption because he has neglected certain other important factors. Nowadays, technology itself is closely associated with global finance, trade, politics and culture, which ultimately impinge upon different national ideologies. The current global situation indicates that the Western industrial countries, which monopolise these technologies, are the real global players, controlling global politics, finance and strategic situations around the world. These are the 'draftsmen' of global maps and the makers and breakers of Third World countries. They are also the providers of arms and chemical weapons for the longest war in recorded history, the eight-year conflict between Iran and Iraq. They are responsible for the emergence of Israel and East Timor and the disintegration of Yugoslavia and Somalia, and the continued imposition of sanctions against the innocent children of Iraq. These are but only a few examples of their immense global power (Chossudovskey, 1998, Armstrong, 2000, Saif, 2000).

From Colonisation to Globalisation

To get a clearer insight into today's traumatic and troubled world, especially with reference to the developing countries, it is vital to look at the phenomenon of the modern European colonisation process, which began in the fifteenth century and has continued to evolve into a more sophisticated form up to the present day. This process has resulted in the emergence of certain patterns and forces that have re-moulded the entire world over the last few centuries. The developing countries, which prior to the demise of the Soviet bloc were also referred to as Third World countries, consist of the bulk of the earth's population, as well as the bulk of its miseries and deprivations. This part of the world reflects various common characteristics. These include political turmoil and instability; perpetual economic crises and poverty; lack of resources for the adequate implementation of justice, illiteracy, armed conflicts, short life expectancy, high population growth, cultural and identity crises, weak and scarce public institutions, massive corruption, and above all crippling debts. Besides these factors they also suffer from a general inability to put their own house in order and effectively manage their own resources, assets and problems, by themselves. Regardless of their respective national statuses, they remain, for all practical purposes, colonies of one imperialist power or the other.

The process of colonisation began when Europeans set out to explore new sea routes with the ultimate goal of accumulating the wealth of India, China and the rest of the world. Pioneered by Portuguese explorers such as Vasco de Gama (1498), who set out to explore Africa and Asia, it was the Dutch, English and French who were to eventually reap the harvest of Portuguese (and Spanish) enterprises. Two main factors provided the driving force for these expensive expeditions; the evolution and establishment of financial support mechanisms funded by the governments and entrepreneurs of Europe; and the technological improvements in shipbuilding and development of navigational instruments.

The global expansion of Western Europe between the 1760s and 1870s differed in several ways from the expansion and the colonialism of previous centuries. Concurrent with the rise of the Industrial Revolution (1760s), and the continued spread of industrialisation in the empire-building countries, came a shift in the strategy of trade across the colonial world. At the heart of this Western expansionism laid the growing disparity in technologies between those of the leading European nations and those of the rest of the world. Indeed, at the outset the difference between the level of technology in Europe and some of the regions on other continents was not especially great in the early part of the eighteenth century.

Later on, the gap between the technologically advanced countries and the rest of the world began to rapidly increase, despite the diffusion of modern technology by colonial powers. Apart from their superiority in terms of armaments, weaponry and military expertise, advances in communications and transportation also became important tools for consolidating foreign rule over extensive territories. Indeed, it was communication technologies and the production of armaments that were to have the most significant impact on the way the British managed distant colonies such as India.

From 1876 to 1914 there were six great powers in the world: Great Britain, Russia, France, Germany, USA and Japan, as well as two secondary powers: Holland and Belgium. These powers succeeded in dividing the world, according to their military might, into zones of influence (Latouche, 1996). Furthermore, there also existed a number of semi-colonised countries such as Iran, Turkey and China. These semi-colonised countries often found themselves in a worse situation than those countries that had been directly colonised. Their political leaders, if they had not been hand picked by the colonial masters, had to operate under a policy of bribery and intimidation, a situation that always proved more beneficial to the colonial powers than the national interests of the colonised. Iran was a case in point. The signing of the Reuter's agreement in the nineteenth century proved more beneficial to British colonial interests than Iranian national interests in that it gave the former more control over India via telegraphic lines that ran through Iran. The increase in business interests and the expansion of trade made communication a vital necessity, and insult was added to injury in this case when the cost of building the telegraphic line was paid for out of the Persian government treasury (Read, 1992). The general policy in colonised and semi-colonised countries was not only to procure and transfer the raw material needed for the manufacturing economy in the West, but also to use the carrot and stick approach to finance their total domination of the peoples in the colonies. It is noteworthy here, that after the battle of Plassy (1775) for instance, the British waged more or less continuous warfare against the Indian people, taking over and controlling more and more of the country. However, the irony is that, the financing and even the military power used for this prolonged undertaking came mainly from India itself (Asghar, 1989; Khalid, 1995, Kamran, 1996).

Naturally, events differed from territory to territory and from time to time, being influenced by the conditions unique to each area, but the drive for expansion remained persistent, as were the pressures to achieve the greatest possible advantages out of the resulting opportunities. By 1914, the colonial powers had succeeded in extending their colonies to cover over 85 percent of the earth's surface. Economic and political control by the leading powers stretched almost across the entire globe. In addition to direct rule, other means of domination were also exercised in the form of spheres of influence, special commercial treaties and the subordination of debtor nations (Kharl, 1997).[1] The question that emerges is one of how to assess the impact of colonisation and the various strategies of subjugation used by the colonisers? It is important to mention here that in 1813, the British Parliament passed a 'Charter Act' which proved of great significance in the history of India. One of this Act's three main elements was to teach Christianity and Western culture to the Indians (Nurullah and Naik, 1951:72-76). This Act was passed after a long debate in the British Parliament and was initiated into law as result of a document presented by Charles Grant (member of parliament) who was also the Chairman of the Board of Directors for the East India Company. Nurullah and Naik (1951:70) argued that during his (Grant's) career with the East India Company, and throughout his tenure as a parliamentarian, he tried his utmost to convince the English people of 'the utterly *immoral* and wretched conditions of Indian society.' In his opinion it was in the interest of Britain to change, in piecemeal fashion, the ideological basis of life in India and the religion of its people. Towards this end, he proposed a strategy of 'silent evolution' that began by teaching English to the Indians, then changing their culture and finally their religion. In his view, this evolution 'would have great and happy effects upon them [Indians], and effects honourable and advantageous for us' (Jalebi, 1953:23).[2]

This was the reason that English was introduced to privileged Indians, and which lead Lord Macaulay to declare, in his famous 'Minutes on Education', that: 'We must at present do our best to form a class who may be interpreters between us and the millions whom we govern – a class of persons Indian in blood and colour, but English in taste, in opinions, in morals and in intellect' (Nurullah and Naik, 1951:113)[3]. The primary aim of this undertaking was therefore to filter the colonial ideology down through this class of persons to the general masses (Sharp, 1922:102-17). Habibi (1967:33) argues that a crucial part of this policy was the fact that the teaching of science, technology, economic and politics was not introduced in the educational system of the colonies, rather the emphasis was laid on English literature, philosophy and culture. As a result, students were able to recite the history of King Alfred or the contents of an Oxford textbook but learned nothing of their own background or culture.

The above example reflects the fact that the primary objective of colonisers was to spread their own culture and, to secure properly trained public servants who would work obediently for their colonial master. The impact of the imposition of foreign culture is well described by Cabral (1997:171) who states that 'the experience of colonial domination shows that in their effort to perpetuate exploitation, the colonisers not only create a system to repress the cultural life of the colonised people, they also provoke and develop the cultural alienation of a part of the population. Thus a considerable part of the population assimilates the coloniser's mentality, considers itself culturally superior to its own people and ignores or looks down upon their cultural values.' Similar views have also been expressed by Weiner (Tachau, 1974:62) who argued that 'colonial governments paid no attention to the teaching of a national language or culture. We are all familiar with the fact that educated Vietnamese, Indonesians, Nigerians, Indians, and Algerians were educated in French, English, and Dutch rather than in their own languages and traditions.'

In the current era, the important issue to note, from the developing nations' point of view, is the fact that the original colonisers are back, with arrogance and renewed sense of purpose that has become strengthened and accelerated following the demise of Soviet bloc. As a result, most of the serious crises that have emerged in the world involve either the direct or indirect interests of these same colonial powers. This discussion of historical background shows that, depending on context, there is a variety of meanings for catchwords like; terrorism, democracy, human rights, justice and environmental preservations. Certain events such as the Gulf War (including its ecological damage, mass-killings, the ethnic cleansing in Europe and continued sanctions on Iraq), the collapse of the BCCI,[4] the war in Bosnia, and the nuclear issue, all take on different meanings when seen from this perspective. The most devastating global events of the last century – World War I and II, the only nuclear attacks on civilians in the history of warfare – were all caused by colonial powers.

Is the present form of globalisation helpful in promoting global peace and prosperity? In the American context, the former US Secretary of State, Henry Kissinger provides one possible answer to this question. In his view: 'It is America's dilemma that we are the most preponderant country that ever existed – in every respect: militarily, economically and in terms of cultural attractiveness. American culture is imitated all over the world. On the other hand, the American people do not consider themselves imperialists. When American leaders intervene around the world they act in the name of what they believe to be universal principles. One should call this a delusion. But it is a fact of practical life. ... I do not think that American hegemony is good for America, nor for Europe' (*Dawn*, 9 April 2000).

The United Nations has also expressed some dissatisfaction with the process of globalisation. It argues that 'geographic barriers may have fallen for communications, but a new barrier has emerged, an invisible barrier that is linked by a world-wide-web, embracing the connected, and silently – almost imperceptibly – excluding the rest.' It further argues that 'markets can go too far and squeeze the non-market activities so vital for human development. Fiscal squeezes are constraining the provision of social services. A time squeeze is reducing the supply and quality of caring labour. And an incentive squeeze is harming the environment. Globalisation is also increasing human insecurity as the spread of global crime, disease and financial volatility outpaces actions to tackle them' (UNDP, 1999).

Mark Malloch Brown, the head of UNDP, supports the arguments of his institution by revealing that: 'Sixty countries have been getting steadily poorer since 1980. The losers from globalisation are both a huge human and political waste and the sources of disappointment and often tragedy for themselves and the families that depend upon them' (UNDP, 1999). These arguments are also shared by Kirn (*Time*, 24 April 2000) who writes: 'It [globalisation] has a sinister ring, like a euphemism from the same technocrats who gave us "downsizing" during the Reagan years and "pacification" during Vietnam.

The term conjures up futuristic vision of a vast, implacable economic process steamrollering their way across the earth, levelling forests, languages and customs without regard for puny individuals. Globalisation: right or wrong, it sounds unstoppable.' It was possibly as a result of such statements that the concerns of Pope John Paul where raised leading him to state that: 'New realities, which are forcefully affecting the productive process, such as the globalisation of finance, of the economy, of commerce and of work, should never be allowed to violate the dignity and centrality of human beings. I feel very close in spirit to people who are forced to live in a poverty which offends their dignity and blocks them from sharing the goods of the earth and forcing them to feed themselves with what falls from the table of the rich' (*Dawn*, 2 May 2000).

Robert Samuelson (*Herald Tribune*, 4 January 2000) rightly states that 'globalisation is a double edge sword' – it is a powerful vehicle for economic growth, and at the same time is an assault on national sovereignty that easily erodes local cultures and threatens social stability. The most pressing question facing the nation state at the dawn of the twenty-first century is the question of control; the multinational or the nation state'. Today nation-state is at the mercy of multi-national corporations. These corporations go for the best deal they can get from the states around the world. Their motive is 'profit' rather than national loyalty or human concern. Thus, unfortunately, the main focus is not on ecological issues, droughts, famines, global warming or basic human rights, rather it is profit and greed which dominates global affairs. This situation creates several problems in the world and promotes further deprivation. In fact, it is a vicious circle in which various factors are mutually supportive to worsen the global situation.

The Widening Gap between Rich and Poor

The above discussion reflects the widening gulf between rich and poor, have and have-nots. Maddison argues that 'inequalities have been rising steadily for nearly two centuries. An analysis of the long term trends in world income distribution between countries shows that the distance between rich and poor countries was around 3 to 1 in 1820; 11 to 1 in 1913; 35 to 1 in 1950; 44 to 1 in 1973, and, 72 to 1 in 1992' (UNDP, 1999: 38). What is even more startling is the fact that the British, in 1820, had an income around six times that of the Ethiopians in 1992. Similar trends can also be seen at an individual level, where this gap is increasing even faster.

Forbes Magazine reveals that in 1994, the world's top 200 richest people owned total assets worth US$ 440 billion, while four year later in 1998, the same people owned US$ 1042 billion (around 59% growth rate per annum). The report further reveals that the assets of the three richest people in the world were more than the combined GNP of all the least developed countries put together, while the assets of the 200 richest people were more than the combined income of 41 percent of the world's total population. This report also suggests that a yearly contribution of only 'one percent' from the wealth of the top 200 rich people could provide universal access to primary education for all (UNDP, 1999: 38).

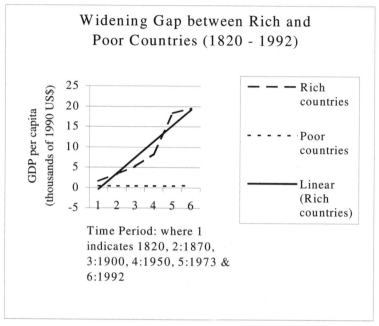

Source: Angus Maddison (1995) in UNDP (1999: 38).

The State of the Muslim World – Past and Present

'Many sociologists have put forward the notion that religion in the contemporary Western world has become increasingly privatised' (Beyer, 1996). In other words, religion, in the context of the secularised modern world, has become an individual rather than a collective matter of concern (Parsons, 1966:125-46, Berger, 1967:133; Luckmann, 1967:103; Bellah, 1970:20-25). This trend can be seen to be true with regard to the 'West'; however, in the 'East' the situation is somewhat different[5]. Pasha and Samatar (1997:187) have highlighted this point and argued that 'the insertion of a new Islamic consciousness into the daily political life of many Muslim societies is increasingly becoming an incontestable fact. In countries like Iran, Sudan, and Afghanistan, Islamic movements have seized state power. For others, such as Algeria, Egypt, Tunisia, and Turkey, there is deadly intensity with high stakes as numerous civil associations define themselves as Islamic and, as a result, violently challenge the legitimacy of political authority. Even in less contested countries (e.g., Morocco, Pakistan, Indonesia), Islamic consciousness assumes a more prominent place in the articulation and making of political life.'

Here it needs to be emphasised that there are two main aspects of globalisation in relation to its economic perspective, i.e., global organisation of production and global finance. The first aspect deals with the complex network of the transnational system relating to issues of production and consumption while the second aspect relates to the transaction of money and lending. This in turn has lead to the emergence of two major phases of globalisation: i) the internationalisation of the state; and, ii) the restructuring of national societies and the emergence of a global social structure (Cox, 1993:259-89). For Muslims these two phases are experienced differently from that which takes place in the rest of the world. Their first phase is their common history and culture, based primarily upon a shared religion, and the second phase is the contemporary age and its developments from which they feel alienated. The realisation of the need for harmonisation with the current globalisation process and a general desire to bridge this widening gap has lead to the emergence of various modern Muslims organisations.

Until the first quarter of the nineteenth century, Muslims remained more or less united under the umbrella of the Caliphate. After its collapse the vast Muslim empires disintegrated and new independent states emerged on the global map. In this changed environment, a series of efforts were made by these states to establish a central institution to fill the resultant gap. In August 1969, the arson damage to the *Al-Aqsa* mosque in Jerusalem outraged Muslims all over the world. Two months after this incident a conference, attended by 24 of the 55 Muslim countries, was held in Rabat (Morocco). Shortly afterwards, in March 1970, a meeting of the foreign ministers of all Muslim countries was held in Jeddah, resulting in the creation of the Organisation of Islamic Countries (OIC) (Abdullah al Ahsan, 1988:18). Since its creation, the membership of OIC has doubled (Bhuyan, 1996:233-35). In principle the OIC's charter is based upon the concept of *Ummah*,[6] while in reality it operates under the idea of national sovereignty borrowed from Western secular thought. The concept of *Ummah* is limited to the level of mutual cooperation among Muslim countries. This contradiction in its Charter is in itself a sign of the organisations weakness, which has resulted in its failure to solve the various political and economic problems that beset the Muslim World. However, in spite of this weakness, it is a well-established institution and provides a base, and a sense of solidarity in the fragmented Islamic bloc. Muslims all over the world feel some satisfaction when they see their leaders sitting together to discuss the problems of Muslim *Ummah* (Husain, 1995: 209).

It should be emphasised here that the globalisation phenomenon relies on three crucial factors, i.e., i) international politics, ii) international trade and financing; and, iii) the media. In this context, and under the framework of the OIC, there are two top-level political institutions, the Islamic Summit Conference and the Foreign Ministers Conference. Two other important commercial institutions – the Islamic Development Bank (IDB), based in Jeddah, and the Islamic Centre for the Development of Trade (ICDT), located in Casablanca, - were established in 1970 and 1981, respectively. With regard to the media, once again, two main institutions dominate – the International Islamic News Agency (IINS) and the Islamic States Broadcasting Organisation (ISBO). The question remains as to how effective these institutions are in their designated roles.

Unfortunately, Muslim political institutions have not been very successful in solving any major problems befalling Muslims. From the Soviet invasion in Afghanistan to its current crises, from the Iran-Iraq War to the Gulf War and from the problems of the Southern Filipino's Muslim community (Choudhury, 1998:197) to the Kosovo crises; no effective measures have been implemented in order to solve these problems. The same is also true of trade among Muslim countries, which only amounts to some 10 percent of total world trade (Choudhury, 1998:196). This situation has gone unchanged for several years, as evidenced by the following figures from 1991; intra-Islamic country trade only accounts for between eight and nine percent of their total trade, compared to 60 percent with the European Community, 34 percent with US-Canada and 28 percent with the European Free Trade Association (Shakweer, 1996:131-59). Furthermore, the improving trends that have been observed in the real per capita GDP of Muslim countries, and generally heralded as a sign of economic improvement, have been neutralised by their dependence on foreign loans. The media, which is a major component of globalisation and plays a key role in moulding global opinion for a particular cause, has completely neglected the Muslim World (Uddin, 1995:101-28). This is one of the reasons given for the narrow spectrum of activities covered by the news agencies of the Muslim World and why they have failed to establish a common network.

Notes:

[1] The history of South Asia reveals that the interest of Western countries in the vast Mughal empire in India was mainly due to its wealth. At first the British arrived in India as traders and then in December 1600, the East India Company was established, initially as a commercial organisation but later on it began to take part in local politics of the sub-continent. The actual foundations of the British Empire were laid with Clive's victory in the Battle of Plassey (1775).

[2] Culture and language were the most important factors in the colonisers drive to influence and dominate a nation. The French and British always used language as the first tool with which to divide and rule their colonies.

[3] Similar views have also been expressed by a former French Governor General of French Africa, who clearly described the goals of colonial powers. He said: 'Political and economic interests have imposed a two-fold task on our work in education. On the one hand, we must train indigenous cadres to become our auxiliaries in every area and ensure ourselves of a meticulously chosen elite. We must also educate the masses to bring them closer to us and transform their way of life. From the political standpoint we must make known our intention of bringing people to the French way of life (Rahnema and Bawtree, 1997: 153). J.B Say, is of the opinion that enlightened nations possess a superior civilisation and savage civilisations possess an inferior one. Therefore, the inhabitants of the latter were somewhat passive and resigned, had a marked preference for leisure and were incapable of any rational reflection and scientific activity. In his words: 'It is in the interest of the human species that the advanced European nations must keep, and even increase, their influence in Asia. ... It is evident that with its despots and superstitions, Asia has no good institutions to lose but she could gain many good ones from the Europeans (Say, 1968: 311).

[4] This is one of the most important financial institutions in the world, and one in which the investors from the Muslim World owned the bulk of shares.

[5] In fact, religion or in other words religious symbolism, is something that no people and no nation could divest itself of as it forms an integral part of their nationalist credo. In several, if not most, Muslim countries, public functions begin with a recitation from the Qura, and an invocation to Almighty Allah. Even 'secular' Egypt under President Anwar Sadaat found it expedient to utilise Islamic symbols and slogans extensively during the Ramdan War of October 1973. Code-named 'Badr', it was launched on the 10th Ramdan, with 'Allahu Akbar' as its battle cry. Egyptian military success was termed an 'Islamic Victory'. Seven years later, during the Iran-Iraq war (1980-88), the secular Bathist Saddam Hussain, wrapped himself in Arab and Islamic robes,

describing the war as another Qadisiya. During the Gulf War (1991), Shah Ahmad Noorani (the leader of Jam'iat-ul-Ulma-il-Islam in Pakistan) was enlisting volunteers on Baghdad's behalf, professing their mission to be the defence of 'Islam'. Zulfikar Ali Bhutto (1928-79), an avowed socialist, shrewdly included Islam as one of the main pillars of his Pakistan People's Party, and strategically presented his 'Islamic Socialism' and *Masawaat*-i-Mohammadi as the slogans with which to convert the country into a socialist state. It is noteworthy that although religious symbolism is generally associated with the East; the West has also shown itself capable of invoking religion in certain circumstances. The national symbols (such as flags, coats of arms, and military honours) and ceremonies of several Western nations – such as Britain, Switzerland, Denmark, Norway, Sweden, Finland, Iceland and Greece – tend to be religious in origin, format and connotation. They represent various adaptations of the cross. Indeed, the cross itself, has been shown to be the most important and potent religious symbol throughout the annals of Christianity. Beyond the concept of religious symbolism some Western flags, like that of Britain, even signify religious events. The British flag contains a triple cross: the red cross represents England's patron-saint, St. George, the diagonal red cross Ireland's patron-saints, while the diagonal white cross on the blue stands for Scotland's patron-saint, St. Andrew, and the diagonal form of his martyrdom. Likewise, the crowns and orbs of European monarchs feature a cross as its most distinctive symbol. At another level, the highest military honour in Britain (Victoria Cross), Germany (Iron Cross) and elsewhere, all contain or exhibit some reference to the cross. Another example is the Western-sponsored, international welfare organisation the Red Cross. The Order of Saint Andrew, Russia's highest decoration is also religious in orientation.

[6] In Islamic philosophy, *Ummah* is a community of law based on certain principles. It is composed of all the followers of the Prophet Mohammad (*mpbuh*). In other words, it is an Islamic brotherhood based on shared responsibility.

2

Under-development
and the Muslim World

Since the 1950s the World has been, for the most part, divided between two super powers, capitalist, denoted by the Free World, and communist, referring to those countries that were under Soviet influence. After the Bandung conference in 1955, another world title emerged. Referred to as the Third World, it formed neither part of the capitalist world nor the pro-Soviet bloc. During the 1950s, the US government employed all of its efforts in attempting to prevent the spread of socialism in the Third World. The First World (i.e., the West, which now encompass all countries with advanced industrial economies and democratic governments), was in direct contrast to zone of industrial communism, with its geographical centre of gravity situated in the Soviet Union, that became known as the Second World. The contest between these two primary worlds formed the central dynamic of post-war global history and relations. All other countries, which encompassed the largest part of the world, fell into a residual category that came to be known as the Third World, the 'developing world' or the 'South'. What then are the major differences between the First and the Third Worlds? At the junction of the twentieth and the twenty-first centuries, only around one fifth of the world's total human population lives in the First World, yet this proportion controls more than 85 percent of all global resources. By contrast, almost one third of the global population lives in the Third World under conditions well below the poverty line, unable to have two meals a day or even acquire the basic facilities for shelter and health care (UNDP, 1998:16-45; UNDP, 1999:25-44). This has given rise to a situation where crime, vandalism and social tensions are increasing and a daily fact of life in these areas.[1] Thomas and Crow (1997:4) have argued that: 'The developing countries (or the Third World), are home to the majority of the earth's population, some three billion people. The term Third World is used to describe a range of countries as diverse as Nigeria and Nepal, Peru and Papua New Guinea. The relationship between the First and Third Worlds (or North and South) profoundly affects both communities. The North consumes fruit grown on the plantations of the Caribbean, fuel extracted from the oilfields of the Middle East, electronics assembled in the factories of Southeast Asia, and clothes spun from cotton on the Indian subcontinent. Likewise, Asian audiences await the latest American 'blockbuster', West African emulates the fashions of Paris, and Latin Americans hope to own a foreign car.'

Another 'World' – The Muslim World

This is only one dimension of the reality, the more important factors, such as the huge discrepancies in living standards, widespread poverty, illiteracy, hunger, famine, human insecurities and instabilities, form the dominant characteristics of the gap between the First and the Third World as seen in any global report emanating from the World Bank or UNDP. A careful examination of the present division of the world, arising as a result of the globalisation process, makes it clear that cultural identity has become one of the most critical issues of debate.

Furthermore, it is necessary to add another category to the current categorisation of the world, as the above global division is no longer sustainable. Within the Third World there exists another important 'world' – the Muslim World. While drawing a picture of the contemporary Muslim World, AbūSulaymān (1994:1) provided the following definition: 'Internally weak, relatively backward, frustrated, conflict-ridden, suffering from internal tensions, and often controlled and abused by foreign powers, the Muslim World is in a state of crisis. For Muslims, all modern history is a tragedy. At an earlier time, during the sweeping revolution of Islam, Muslims were the custodians of civilisation and both the centre and masters of the civilised world. But at present, the Muslim polity is neither master nor partner, and both Muslims and Islam are often regarded in world politics as little more than problematic. How did such a state of affairs come about, and in what ways can the Muslim peoples alter this condition? In Muslim countries it is customary to blame external powers and imperialism for all manners of ills. Although this habit may point up many of the grievances and obstacles Muslims face, it cannot explain the internal cause of the ills. These ills put in motion a process of decay that dissipated the internal powers of the Muslim World. The resultant weakness brought external powers into the picture, complicating the difficulties. The problem of the external factors, along with the complications they caused for the Muslim World, cannot be dealt with before the internal factors are fully understood.'

In the words of Sarwar (1997:9): 'The Muslim World is today perched on the horns of an excruciating dilemma. It has been subjected to colonial domination for a very long time and has recently extricated itself from the West's stranglehold. It is heartening to note that in its struggle against colonialism, it has achieved major successes. However, it has yet to go a long way in breaking intellectual, psychological, cultural, economic and technological chains. The crisis that engulfed the Muslim World during the last three centuries, can be attributed both to external and internal factors.' One of the main problems for the Muslim World is the fact that Islam is the most misunderstood religion in the West – a religion that stands for peace and justice has been misinterpreted as a religion of war and fanaticism (Naqvi, 1984:5-33). According to Ahmad (1995:5-6), a famous Muslim thinker: 'The Muslim World which has suffered at the hands of the West in the past and which remains even today weak materially, economically, technologically and militarily, is now being projected as a threat to the West. Their efforts to rediscover their identity and set their own house in order are looked upon as a challenge to the West. The Frankenstein of 'Islamic fundamentalism' is being seen in the innocuous efforts of the Muslims to activate the democratic process and seek self-reliance. From former presidents Richard Nixon (*Seize the Moment*) and Ronald Reagan (*An American Life*) to intellectuals like Francis Fukuyama (*The End of History and the Last Man*) and columnists like Richard Pfaff and others are playing on the theme of Islam's threat to the West. They are all drum-beating as if a spectre is haunting Europe and America, the spectre of Islamic fundamentalism. This is a one sided war. Yet the politicians, journalists and media men, even some scholars are the party to the projection of this scare-mongering scenario.'

The above views are also shared by an American scholar who has criticised the Western media for painting a negative picture of Islam and the Muslims. He states that: 'As there is very little knowledge about Islam in America, when news about Osama Bin Laden and the Taliban came into media, Americans got an impression of Muslims based on extremism and antagonism. In reality, it is a political and sociological phenomenon and the people believe what is being poured into their minds' (Ernst, 2000). In the events surrounding the Persian Gulf War and its aftermath, the level of inaccuracy by the Western media in reporting on the Islamic World and Muslims in general, resulted in the portrayal of the Islamic World in a highly negative and xenophobic fashion. Those living in the West were not spared the full brunt of 'Islamophobia'.[2] Despite common theological roots and centuries of interaction, Islam's relationship with the West has often been marked by mutual ignorance, stereotyping, contempt and conflict. Ancient rivalries and modern day conflicts have so accentuated differences as to completely obscure the shared theological roots and visions of the Judeo-Christian-Islamic tradition (Esposito, 1995:25).

This is one of the main reasons posited as an explanation for the fact that the Muslim World is internally weak, unstable, and dependent on the First World. This situation can be judged from the fact that the total GDP of all Muslim countries put together accounts for only half the GDP of Germany and only a quarter of Japan's in spite of the fact that the Muslim countries produce most of the world's oil (World Bank, 1999). In addition to accusing others, Muslim scholars have been misleading themselves by constant reference to a magnificent past and a utopian future which fails to confront the realities of the modern world where rational and national considerations leave little room for sentimental responses. The present Muslim states have also failed in their efforts to create credible and inspiring role models. The ruling authorities of the Muslim World often misinterpret the realities of the situation by ignoring the vital issues of poverty, hunger, inadequacy and widespread illiteracy that limit social justice and economic progress. Therefore, in many Muslim countries social problems are so deeply rooted as to leave the state in a position of complete vulnerability.

The ultimate impact of such social weaknesses is not only internal, but also adversely affects the overall global position of that country's standing in the world. Pakistan is a case in point. This country 'is in the grip of a grim crises but for Pakistanis, this is not a new phenomenon. This frustration is now broadening into cynicism and people find themselves on the 'horn of the dilemma' (Sarwar, 1997:97-106). Karachi, with its industrial establishments and international financial institutions, has always been Pakistan's largest industrial, commercial and business centre, and the biggest contributor to the national exchequer. However, this has all changed with crime now becoming Karachi's fastest growing industry. During 1999, over 650 people were killed in political, sectarian and other violence, of which 90 were city nobles and dignitaries. Under such circumstances, foreign trade and investment by transnational corporations has rapidly fallen and almost disappeared (*Dawn*, 14 April 2000).

How Big is the Muslim World?

According to 1998 estimates, out of a total global population of 5.87 billion some 1.31 billion (22.2%) were Muslims.[3] Similarly, out of the 103 million Km^2 of geographic area that covers the world, Muslims occupy some 30.5 million Km^2 (22.8%). The global map indicates that the Muslim World stretches from North West Africa (Morocco) to South East Asia (Indonesia). It ranges from the Atlantic Ocean to the Pacific, the Mediterranean Sea and Indian Ocean, and Muslims control the main gateways of the world's trade and commerce arteries, such as the straits of Gibraltar, Bosphorus, Hormuz, Malaka and the Suez Canal (Tabibi, 1997:10-19). However, the role that Muslim countries play in global affairs are non what so ever. Even after the withdrawal of Soviet Union from Afghanistan, the leadership of the Muslim World was not able to bring peace and stability to a war-torn Muslim country.

Table: 2.1. Basic Facts about the Muslim and
the Non-Muslim World

Population and Area	Muslim Countries		Non-Muslim Countries	
	Total (million)	% of the world	Total (million)	% of the world
Total Muslim population	1024	17.4	284	4.8
Total Non-Muslim population	174	3.0	4394	74.7
Area (000 Km$^{2)}$	30,442	22.8	103,058	77.2

Source: Computed from: World Bank, 1999; Castello-Cortes, 1999; New
Internationalist Publications Ltd., 2000; Dar, 1999; Sarwar, 1994;
The Economist Intelligence Unit (various); CIA, 2000; UNDP,
1999.

It was further estimated that Muslim countries produce more
than two thirds of the world's oil, 70 percent of its rubber, 75
percent of its jute, 67 percent of its spices, two-thirds of all palm
oil, and half of all tin and phosphate. In addition, having a vast
number of gas reserves, they also produce a large quantity of the
world's cotton, tea, coffee, wool uranium, manganese, cobalt
and many other commodities and minerals. Geographically,
these countries occupy the most strategically important areas in
the world with nearly, 60 percent of the Mediterranean Sea
bounded by Muslim countries, and with the Red Sea and the
Persian Gulf exclusively located within the Muslim region
(Sarwar, 1994).

Human Deprivation

During the recent past, several developing countries have made
considerable economic progress. This can be seen most clearly
in the figures showing increases in income and the rising trend

in consumption. The broader global picture reflects increased improvements in life expectancy and educational attainments (World Bank, 1999). In contrast to these achievements, there still exists a large number of people, particularly in the developing world, who are living below the poverty line. The *Human Development Report 1999* states that 'global technological breakthroughs offer greater potential for human advancements and for the eradication of poverty – but not with today's agendas' (UNDP, 1999:6). International comparisons of poverty data entail both conceptual and practical problems. Different countries have different definitions of poverty, and consistent comparisons between different countries are difficult. Given these problems, the most commonly used method of analysis by the World Bank is that which rests on 'purchasing power parities', commonly known as PPPs (World Bank, 2000:65).

Table 2.2 presents a comparative picture of the Muslim and the Non-Muslim worlds. It is noteworthy that with regard to the basic indicators, the Muslim World remains far behind the Non-Muslim World. The World Bank figures reveal that nearly a quarter of the population in the developing and the transitional economies are living below the poverty line. However, the analysis with respect to the Muslim countries indicates that nearly one-third of the population of the low-income Muslim countries are living below the poverty line. By comparison, the comparative figure for low-income Non-Muslim countries was one-fourth. As mentioned previously, it needs to be emphasised that the concept of poverty differs in both the developing and the developed worlds. This arises from the fact that in the former, people below the poverty line are deprived of the basic necessities of life, whilst in the latter people are provided with these basics through social benefits and necessary financial assistance form the state.

The figures show the overall quality of life in the Muslim World to be much lower than that of the Non-Muslin World. Moreover, as the population growth rate in the Muslim World is considerably higher than that in the Non-Muslim World, these statistics also indicate that more resources will be needed by the former if the gap between the two is not to widen even further in the future. But the question remains, how given current circumstances can the desired goals of development be achieved? Unless immediate and adequate measures are adopted, the task of attaining the required level of development seems almost impossible. This is highlighted by the fact that the overall GDP growth rate in the Muslim World during the past two decades has been negative when compared with the Non-Muslim World. Even within the Non-Muslim World, the difference between high and low income countries is quite clear with the former having a high GDP growth rate while the latter exhibit a small growth rate. This situation also indicates the various countries that are reaping the maximum benefits from the globalisation process.

The negative affects of the above situation further aggravate due to the lack of competent and honest leadership in the Muslim World. The high level of corruption, mismanagement of resources and internal instability in several Muslim countries plays its role to keep them underdeveloped. One outcome of this situation is the out-flow of human and financial capitals. It is common knowledge that rather than investing in their own countries, a large number of extremely wealthy families in the Muslim World keep their savings in western banks which leads to a shortage of financial capital and means that Muslim countries are bound to borrow from international financial institutions even on some occasions by accepting inhumane conditionalities which raise their debt burden and keep their masses below the poverty line. Due to the lack of investment and saving, this situation also promotes high unemployment which encourages out-migration of talented people from the Muslim World. Resultantly, these countries are then forced to hire foreign experts form western industrial countries on the payment of high amounts of foreign exchange. If the leadership of the Muslim World could realise the severity and the nature of this problem, the living conditions of their masses could be much improved.

Table: 2.2. Basic Indicators about the Muslim and
the Non-Muslim Worlds

Item	Muslim World		Non-Muslim World	
	High income countries	Low income countries	High income countries	Low income countries
Population living below poverty line (%)	..	32.6	7.6	25.3
Per capita GDP (US$)	9,913	645	25,180	2,512
GDP growth rate (%)	-0.67	-0.17	2.81	1.11
Literacy rate (%)	76	57	98	79
Life expectancy (years)	70	58	77	64
Population growth rate (%)	2.1	2.2	0.5	1.3
Population without safe water (%)	18	34	9	31
No of Doctors per 100,000 persons	126	87	268	138

Source: Computed from: World Bank, 1999/2000; UNDP, 1999.

Note: The division of high and low-income countries, both in case of the Muslim and the Non-Muslim worlds is based on the World Bank and UNDP reports from 1999. In this division, high and upper-middle income countries are considered as 'high-income countries', while lower-middle and lower-income countries are categorised as 'low-income countries'. Thus, according to this classification, Bahrain, Brunei, Gabon, Kuwait, Lebanon, Libya, Malaysia, Oman, Qatar, Saudi Arabia, Turkey and UAE are classified as 'high-income Muslim countries' while the rest are deemed to be low-income Muslim countries. In the case of Non-Muslim countries, Australia, Austria, Belgium, Canada, Denmark, Finland, France, Germany, Ireland, Italy, Japan, Luxembourg, Netherlands, New Zealand, Norway, Portugal, Spain, Sweden, Switzerland, United Kingdom and the United States are all grouped as 'high-income countries' while the rest fall into the category of 'low-income countries'. It is important to note that in the case of 'high-income Muslim countries' (with the exception of Turkey, Gabon, Lebanon and Malaysia), most are oil producers while in the category of 'high-income Non-Muslim countries' all are: i) members of the world's Developmental Assistance Committee (DAC), ii) major creditors, aid providers, and the controllers of the activities of the World Bank and the IMF, iii) belong to the group of the 'North', iv) are technologically advanced, v) major global players, vi) makers and breakers of global maps, vii) have dominant positions in the United Nations, and, viii) according to various 'Human Development Reports' of the UNDP, are in the top world ranking of 'Human Development Index'. In fact, these are the countries, which are controlling the whole world and gaining the maximum benefits from the present process of globalisation.

Today the Muslim World as a whole faces a number of challenges as evidenced by the serious problems that beset individual Muslim countries. Some of these countries are either facing the problems of civil war or, are engaged in war-like situations. In addition, according to the available statistics, Gambia, Mauritania, Uganda, Kazakhstan, Kyrgyzstan, Turkmenistan and Uzbekistan are among the poorest countries of the world where the majority of the population live well below the poverty line. There are some other countries (e.g., Chad and Tunisia) where per capita GDP is less than US$ 250.

Widespread illiteracy is another major evil in the Muslim World. Niger with its 14 percent literacy rate is the most illiterate country in the world, followed by Burkina Faso (21%) and Gambia (33%). It is also common knowledge that poverty, illiteracy and internal instability adversely affect the state of public health in a country. Thus, the lowest level of life expectancy in the world is also seen in Muslim countries (Afghanistan and Burkina Faso; only 45 year).

Human Development

Mahbub ul Haq, the founder of the concept of 'human development'[4] at the United Nations states that: 'The human development ranks of Islamic countries are generally lower than per capita income ranks, showing that their income has not been fully translated into the lives of their people. The overall Human Development Index (HDI) for 49 Islamic countries is only 0.393, placing the Islamic World in the low human development category (Mahbub ul Haq, 1999:105) In fact, HDI is an aggregate value of life expectancy, adult literacy, mean years of schooling and per capita income. According to the *Human Development Report 1999,* as many as 45 Muslim countries had a lower value of HDI than that of the world average (UNDP, 1999).

The statistics indicated by Mahbub ul Haq rightly point out that in similar income groups, many Muslim countries are far behind their Non-Muslim counterparts in terms of human development. In the following table only two examples are quoted in this regard. The data indicates that within the group of high-income countries with similar income, the HDI world ranking places Qatar in the 41st position as against Australia in 7th position. Similarly, in low-income countries, Iran occupies the 95th position in comparison to Estonia, which is ranked 54th. The literacy rate in Australia and Estonia was 99 percent as compared to Qatar and Iran where these figures were 80 and 73 percent, respectively. This situation indicates that the mismanagement of resources in the Muslim countries is one of the prime reasons for their state of 'human under-development'.

Table: 2.3. Comparison of the Muslim and the Non-Muslim
Countries with Similar Income but Different
Level of Human Development

Country	HDI ranking	GDP per capita (US$)	Life expectancy (years)	Literacy rate (%)
High Income				
• Qatar	41	20,987	71.7	80.0
• Australia	7	20,210	78.2	99.0
Low Income				
• Iran	95	5,817	69.2	73.3
• Estonia	54	5,240	68.7	99.0

Source: UNDP, 1999: 134-35.

Under-Development in the Twenty-first Century

Regarding the above discussion, a simple question arises - what will the state of development in the Muslim World be like in the twenty-first century? Unfortunately, analysis of the global statistics does not present an encouraging picture. It can be argued that during the past decade, various Muslim countries have made some progress with regard to human development but in this age of globalisation and competition, this progress is proving to be insufficient. It is worth noting that out of a total of 56 Muslim countries, only 35 had data available and of these, 33 have fallen down in the HDI world ranking. Furthermore, although some major global players have also fallen down in the world ranking, they still remain among the top countries of the global HDI. The average value of HDI for the Muslim World as a whole has fallen by −33.14 as against 3.05 for the high-income Non-Muslim countries (UNDP, 1999). This situation begs a number of pertinent questions; what will become of the state of human development in the Muslim World during the twenty-first century if this present trend is allowed to continue? Will the existing gap between the Muslim and the Non-Muslim worlds become even more pronounced? Are the major global players responsible for this situation, or is it attributable to the internal weaknesses of the Muslim World itself? And finally, is underdevelopment the root cause of violence, or does violence cause underdevelopment? The coming chapters attempt to explore the answers of these and other similar questions.

With regard to issues of violence and terrorism, which are attributes exclusively accredited to the Muslim World, Syed (1997:189) argues that: 'The origin of terrorism, in fact, lies in economic and political terrorism which has been perpetuated on the developing countries particularly in the Muslim countries (see following diagram). In the past, it was done in the form of imperialism, colonialism, neo-colonialism etc; today it is being done by not resolving outstanding conflicts, fanning the existing ones and creating new conflicts. At the same time these countries are being denied the transfer of technology and scientific know-how with a view to perpetuating technological monopoly and dominance. The value order of most of the Muslim countries is also threatened by the 'new world order' and ensuing trade and economic policies.' Given these circumstances, how can one possibly envisage a smooth process of development for the Muslim World into the new millennium?

Global Politico-Economic Environment Leading to Violence

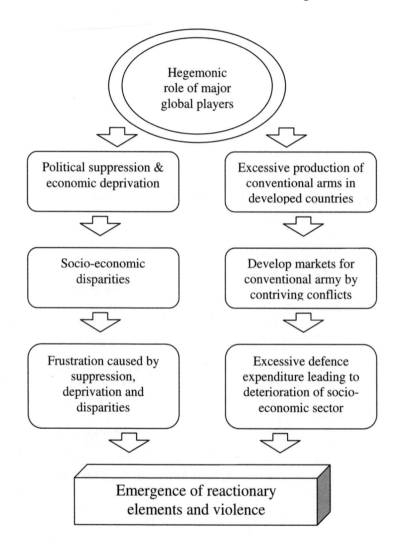

Source: Derived from, Syed, 1997: 211.

Notes:

[1] The total Muslim population in the World is about 1.2 billion, which accounts for almost one quarter of the world's total population. It is impossible for the West to ignore the prevailing conditions in Muslim countries if it is seriously concerned about the process of globalisation. It is important that the economic modernisation occurring throughout the world at present will eventually lead to the weakening of nation-states resulting in religion moving to fill the void caused by the ensuing identity crises. This factor, in conjunction with other developments, shows that further global integration is being replaced by the emergence of new blocs of groups based on new market, ethnic and cultural identities. Since the demise of communism, and the rapid progress of globalisation, a number of economic blocs and regional economic clusters have emerged as significant factors in reinforcing a new cultural identity through the market economy. The Gulf Cooperation Council and the Caspian Sea Economic Market are significant examples of this phenomenon.

[2] Mohammed Mujeeb, a former Lord Mayor of Bradford (UK), was sent a gruesome letter stating that the solution to the 'problem' of Muslims was gas chambers. This particular episode serves as potent reminder of religious intolerance and the anti-Semitism suffered by the Jews at the hands of the Nazis.

[3] This population includes only the Muslim people, irrespective of their place of residence (i.e., Muslim or Non-Muslim countries). However, in the specific case of geographic areas, the figure of 22.8% refers exclusively to Muslim countries.

[4] Late Mahbub ul Haq (1934-1998) served in various high-level capacities, including chief architect of World Bank's focus on poverty reduction strategies and a close associate of the World Bank's President, Robert S. McNamara. He also acted as a Special Advisor to the UNDP Administrator, and is the founder and author of the UNDP's annual Human Development Reports (1990-95).

3

The Infinite Debt Spiral

The current global financial system has created several problems in the world. Many people blame the World Bank and the IMF for the widespread poverty and miseries that exists throughout the Third World. Catherine Caufield (1998: xii) has stated that: 'When I began writing this book [entitled: *Master of Illusion – The World Bank and the Poverty of Nations*], I asked the Bank to supply me with the manifestoes of the completed projects of which it was most proud. As I travelled, I wanted to be able to visit these as well as the many that had been brought to my attention by critics. I repeated my request on several occasions, always receiving the assurance that a list would be sent to me soon. The list, however, never materialised.'

Similarly, the renowned and respected charity organisation, 'Christian Aid' (Madeley *et. al*, 1994: 8, 22), argues: 'Their [the World Bank and IMF] current policies are intended to help poor nations move out of poverty and into economic health. But our stance is: i) their policies are not working for the poor but effectively destroying the lives of many, and we must expose this, ii) their power to dictate to the economies of poor nations is too great, and we must hold them accountable, iii) alternative strategies could be tried, and poor people themselves should have the right to shape their own future, and, iv) between 1982 and 1987, the total foreign debt of developing countries almost doubled, rising from $ 650 billion to $ 1190 billion. High rates of interest on the world market turned this debt into an intolerable burden and diverted resources that the Third World urgently needed in order to develop into industrialised countries.'[1]

Similar views have also been expressed by the New Internationalist Publications Ltd. (1999:74) which states that: 'International negotiations to reduce and eliminate the foreign debt of the Third World have only led to increasing exports of capital and the further indebtedness of the countries affected (as with Sub-Saharan Africa). The wealthy North has established a new form of economic colonialism, a new version of the old "debt bondage".' A recently published report (Jubilee, 2000) showed how, in 1996, Africa paid out US$ 1.31 in debt service for every one dollar it received in grant. The total debt owed by African countries in 1996 was US$ 227 billion, which works out at US$ 379 for every person living on the continent. Altogether, African countries owe 11 percent of the total debt of the developing world, yet they possess only five percent of the income of the entire South. The report also indicates that in 1997, the IMF was expected to disburse five billion dollars in the region whilst at the same time continuing to extract around US$ 700 million annually. At present the debt of 41 highly indebted countries was calculated to amount to a total of US$ 215 billion; a figure which has increased dramatically from 183 in 1990 and 55 in 1980. In this context, the UNDP (1998) predicted that if the external debt of the 20 poorest countries of the world was written off, it could save the lives of 20 million people before the year 2000. In other words it means that uncancelled debt was responsible for the deaths of 130,000 children a week up until the year 2000.

According to Soren Ambrose,[2] the IMF and the World Bank are 'preferred creditors'[3] which gain power over poor countries as the amounts owned to them increase. Similarly, 'structural adjustment programmes' (SAP) which reorient economies, to the benefit of corporate interests, consequently reducing spending on domestic programmes and locally oriented production, are imposed by these institutions on severely indebted countries. The impact of this situation is felt most acutely by the diversion of national resources to debt servicing and the maintenance of SAP's which are designed to transform local economies into a globalised model of production and export aimed at accruing the highest level of hard currency. The SAP linked loans of the IMF and the World Bank are meant to finance the redesigning of governmental, industrial and commercial systems, to enable countries to continue to pay debt servicing. However, SAPs have almost invariably caused an increase in poverty, unemployment and environmental destruction, and have usually led to an increase in the overall size of a country's multilateral debt. The universal failure of the standard SAP recipe has meant that debt and structural adjustment simply end up fuelling one other. One of the major problems in the decision making process of the IMF and the World Bank is their voting system which is based on the percentage of financial contributions made by its members. It means that poor countries have little or no voice while the United States government holds nearly all the decision-making power. Thus, in determining their policy, US Treasury officials seek to maintain leverage over other nations' economic policies.

Another important point is that, in order to qualify for the status of a 'heavily indebted poor country' (HIPC), a country must complete three years under an IMF-designed SAP. Even after that hurdle, the country must fulfil a further three years bound by the recommendations of another SAP before relief on multilateral debt is granted. At the same time, all creditors give matching relief to reduce the country's debt to a 'sustainable' level. The June 1999 G-8[4] summit proposed moving the time frame for the granting of relief so that it would occur upon completion of the first SAP, though the debt could be reinstated if the second SAP was not fulfilled to the IMF's satisfaction. Here, the inhumane paradox is that several poor countries, which are in desperate need of debt relief, so that they can begin to direct resources to social sectors, are first required to demonstrate their willingness to make things worse by starving their people of basic health care, food subsidies and primary education (George, 1990; Payer, 1991; World Bank, 1992; Hansen-Kuhn and Hellinger, 1999).

Globalisation of Debt Trap and the Case of the Muslim World

In July 1999, the G-8 summit in Cologne announced, with great fanfare, a package of enhanced debt relief totalling US$ 100 billion for the poorest counties of the world. By the beginning of the following year's conference in July 2000, only nine countries had received payment, amounting to a mere US$ 15 billion of the total promised package. The question that then arises is why this debt relief package was announced in the first place and why it failed to be fully implemented? In fact, it was in the political and security interests of the most dominant player in the IMF and the World Bank (particularly the US), to support the poorest countries at this particular time. For the past few years there has been growing pressure on rich countries to write off the debts of HIPC. One such pressure group is Jubilee 2000, a UK-based coalition of anti-debt groups, which expressed the view that the Cologne initiative will, in actual terms give a little to some countries but nothing to most. The IMF itself admitted that Mali, for instance, being the eighth poorest country in the world, will pay more in debt service after the Cologne initiative than it did before (Jubilee *2000*, 2000).

The weekly *Economist* (22 July 2000) wrote that a more disturbing development is the fact that some rich countries, notably the United States, have not yet made good on their commitments to finance debt relief. According to Jubilee 2000 (14 July 2000), the G-8 leaders left the island of Okinawa without agreeing on a new deal for debt cancellation. Their final communiqué merely recycled the promises of a year ago, which have already been broken. Similarly, the *Times* newspaper, (24 July 2000) state: 'How badly common sense was lacking in Okinawa is also evident from the fact that while President Clinton pledged 300 million dollars to give children in poor countries "a free school lunch", it was revealed that the total amount which the Japanese spent on the Okinawa summit comes to 735 million dollars – an amount sufficient to pay for twelve million children to go to school.'

UNDP's *Human Development Report 1997* (1997: 7) argued that relief in the debt payment of severely indebted countries could enable them to use these funds for investment and that in Africa alone this relief would be enough to save the lives of 21 million children by 2000, and provide 90 million women and girls with access to basic levels of education. The above suggestion was made in 1997, and lives continue to be lost as the money that should be used for health care is earmarked for debt payments. Under these circumstances many indebted countries are having to pay more on servicing their debt each year than they spend on health care and education. Another important point worth noting is the complete absence of accountability on the part of lenders, the dictated nature of their policies and the imposed conditionalities that create further problems and mass unrest in the loan recipient countries.[5] The question emerges as to whether these global lending institutions, in pursuing their own agendas, possess even a minimum level of concern for the human welfare of the mass poor? Sadly, the answer is in the negative as evidenced by the statement of the leader of the six-member IMF mission, Lazaro E. Molho, at Dhaka: 'We advocate faster reforms. We are not bound to each country's situation' (*Times*, 11 November 2000). To further review this situation, two examples, one from a high and another from low-income Muslim countries are assessed and analysed.

Kuwait is one of the richest countries in the world and does not face the financial challenges besetting many other Third World countries. Unfortunately, after the Gulf crises major global players, particularly the United States, the IMF and the World Bank, have been keen to advise on economic policy in this country. In April 2000, the IMF urged Kuwait to implement economic reforms, charge fees for government services and reduce subsidies. This was in spite of the fact that according to a report in 1999, the IMF itself noted an improvement in the Kuwaiti economy by highlighting figures which showed that the government surplus exceeded 15 percent of GDP. In a country where the majority of the workforce belongs to the expatriate category, and unemployment and poverty are completely absent, it is somewhat strange that the IMF should argue for an increase in economic growth and employment opportunities at the cost of increasing charges on utilities, imposing more tax on various items of daily use, reducing subsidies, and cutting government expenditures. Furthermore, the IMF also urged for the elimination of import duties on various items (*Dawn*, 8 April 2000). Why then are these reforms deemed essential, and why has the IMF urged Kuwait to eliminate import duties? It is common knowledge that throughout Kuwaiti history (with some exceptions), the country has had surplus budgets and these surplus amounts have been invested in American and other Western banks and stock markets. According to a Kuwaiti intellectual who preferred to remain anonymous, the IMF has a secret agenda, to extract every penny from the Kuwaiti economy. The drive to exempt luxury items from import duty adds further credence to this view as most of the items of daily use are imported from the United States.[6]

By comparison, Pakistan is presented here as the prime example of a low-income country. In May 2000, by arguing that it is internationally uncompetitive, the World Bank asked Pakistan to shutdown all of its ailing industrial units. The Bank identified sugar refining, fertiliser, textile and steel industries as the industries it wished to see cease operations. It went even further by asking for the termination of all investment in these areas (*Nation*, 20 May 2000). It needs to be emphasised that agriculture is the largest sector of the Pakistani economy, employing nearly half of its labour force and producing one quarter of its GDP. This sector is also closely linked to the rest of the sectors of the economy and supplies a regular flow of workers to the non-agricultural sectors and is taxed in such a way as to provide inexpensive food to the working classes (Saeed, 1999). Under these circumstances it is not difficult to assess whether the World Bank's actions were based on sincerity, or a desire to leave the country in a volatile state with high unemployment, increased poverty, mass-unrest and an uncertain future.

In this context it is important to mention the interview given by Ken Livingston, the Mayor of London to a local magazine, *New Musical Express*, (April, 2000). He claimed that global capitalism kills more people each year than were killed by Adolf Hitler and held the IMF and the World Bank responsible for causing the death of millions by refusing to ease the Third World's debt burden. Asked by a reader whether he believed that the bosses of these institutions should die painfully in their beds he replied that the IMF and the World Bank as well as the World Trade Organisation (WTO) were appalling institutions that caused people to die unnecessarily because of an unequal international financial system. Susan George estimated that in any year since 1981, between 15 and 20 million people had died unnecessarily from the debt burden because Third World governments have had to cut back on clean water and health programmes to meet their repayments (*Times*, 11 April, 2000). This situation reflects that international financial institutions did not play a positive role in eliminating the widespread human deprivation in the developing countries.

Debt Burden on the Muslim and Non-Muslim Worlds

The comparison of the state of indebtedness of the Muslim and the Non-Muslim worlds highlights some important facts. The following table shows that even high-income Muslim countries are heavily indebted,[7] with the same being true for the per year growth rate of their debts. It was estimated that this growth rate is 27 percent per year. There was no comparison with the growth of national income where the figure was shown to be a negative.[8] With respect to the per capita debt burden, and despite the fact that the low-income Non-Muslim countries have slightly more debt burden as compared to the low-income Muslim countries, the situation does not reflect the real picture unless it is seen in conjunction with the debt burden taken as a percent of GNP and exports.

The figures (table: 3.1) indicate that in comparison to Non-Muslim countries, Muslim countries are bearing around 26 percent more debt burden as a percent of GNP and exports. This situation indicates that the debt problem is comparatively more serious in Muslim countries as there is little money available for developmental and social welfare projects.

There is another important point with regard to the Muslim World which should be mentioned here. In general, in these countries there is a serious lack of concern to fix priorities in the development process. Under the current circumstances, to overcome the immediate problem of high unemployment which further promotes several social problems, Muslim countries should focus on labour intensive technology, particularly in the fields of agriculture, agro-based industry, basic engineering and mining. This would help to strengthen their economic and social infrastructure and provide a solid base for advancement in the field of science and technology which is a capital intensive business. Apart from other positive affects, this process would promote the exports of Muslim countries and help them to reduce the high debt burden.

Table: 3.1. Situation of Indebtedness of the Muslim and the Non-Muslim Worlds

Item	Muslim World		Non-Muslim World	
	High income countries	Low income countries	High income countries	Low income countries
Total debt per capita (US$)	1,564	407	..	444
Debt as a % of GNP	58	61	..	45
Debt as a % of export	83	209	..	154
Per year growth rate of debt (%), 1980-97	27	16	..	18

Source: Computed from: UNDP, 1999, World Bank, 2000.

Out of the total of 38 Muslim countries for which data was available, 34 percent were severely indebted, 37 percent were moderately indebted and 29 percent were in the category of less indebted. Among the high-income countries, Gabon was severely indebted while the other major Muslim countries such as Malaysia and Turkey were classified as moderately indebted. Among the Non-Muslim countries, 36 percent were deemed to be severely indebted, 26 percent moderately indebted, and 38 percent were less indebted. These figures indicate that the proportionate number of Non-Muslim countries in the category of less indebted was higher as compared to Muslim countries. In addition, there are some alarming figures concerning individual Muslim countries. Bahrain, which is considered to be one of the richest countries in the world, was also the world's most heavily indebted country where per capita debt burden was US$ 11,806. It is unclear as to what were the reasons for acquiring such huge amount of loans and their resultant debts.

Debt Burden – A Cross Country Comparison

To further analyse the state of indebtedness, it would be appropriate to present a cross country comparison of some of the selected countries in the Muslim and the Non-Muslim worlds. In table 3.2, four groups of countries are selected for comparison; the first two are the top-most and the second top-most indebted countries, while the other two are of similar income. Bahrain and Argentina occupy the positions of the most indebted countries from the Muslim and the Non-Muslim worlds, respectively. As mentioned earlier, in spite of earning large amounts of petro-dollars, Bahrain is three times more indebted than Argentina. Similarly, Gabon and the Republic of Korea are the second top-most indebted countries of their respective worlds. In the case of Gabon, the per capita debt burden is around half of the per capita GDP. However, the same burden for the Republic of Korea is only around one fourth of its per capita GDP. It is for this reason that Gabon falls into the category of severely indebted countries while the Republic of Korea is in the category of less indebted countries. In the other two groups, Jordan and the Philippines on one hand, and Algeria and Romania on the other, have similar GDP per capita but different debt burdens. In these two groups, both Muslim countries are facing nearly two to three times more debt burden as compared to their Non-Muslim counterparts. Thus, Jordan and Algeria are both categorised as severely indebted countries.

Furthermore, as compared to the Philippines and Romania, both Jordan and Algeria are much further behind in the UNDP's global HDI ranking (UNDP, 2000). This situation reflects the fact that the state of indebtedness and human under-development is much more serious in the Muslim World than the Non-Muslim World. The above facts are also supported by Choudhury (1998:198-99), who presented estimates that show that in case of Muslim countries the aggregate burden of external debt was nearly double the total overall debt burden of the developing countries.

Table: 3.2. Cross Comparison of Indebtedness of the Muslim and the Non-Muslim Countries

Country	Per capita GDP (US$)	Debt per capita (US$)	Indebtedness classification
The top most indebted			
• Bahrain	16,527	11,806	..
• Argentina	10,300	3,423	Severely
The second top most indebted			
• Gabon	7,550	4,284	Severely
• Korea (Rep.)	13,590	3,117	Less
Similar income			
• Jordan	3,450	1,647	Severely
• Philippines	3,520	606	Moderately
Similar income			
• Algeria	4,460	1,030	Severely
• Romania	4,310	475	Less

Source: Computed form: World Bank, 2000; UNDP, 1999.

Debt Servicing

According to Muslim belief, Islam is a complete code of life as it provides guidance with regard to every aspect of life. A similar claim is also made with regard to the economic system. One of the basic and most important characteristics regarding the social economy and the economic system upon which the Quran repeatedly lays stress is that all means and resources are Divinely created (Ahmad, 1976: 3-18, 171-88). Therefore, one of the most important characteristics of Islamic economy is that it is free of interest, as according to Islamic philosophy, interest is neither a trade nor a profit – but a socio-economic evil (Siddiqui, 1983, 1985, 1988, 1996; Khan, 1985, Chapra, 1992, Khan, 1995). Around fourteen hundred years ago, the Quran clearly stated that: 'They say, trade is like interest and Allah has allowed trade and prohibited interest' (2: 275). 'Whatever you pay as interest, so that it may increase in the property of [other] man, it does not increase with Allah' (30: 39).

This leads to the question as to why Islam has prohibited interest? Chapra (2000: 5-20) has provided six rationales for the prohibition of interest in Islam, i.e., i) establishment and implication of justice – a central goal of Islam, ii) need fulfilment, iii) optimum economic growth, iv) full employment, v) equitable distribution, and, vi) economic stability in society. Due to the limited scope of this chapter it is not possible to go into the details of an alternative Islamic economic system as a huge volume of research has already been conducted in this regard. In essence, Islam advocates a system of *Mudarabah* (profit sharing) and *Musharakah* (joint business) where all parties involved in an economic activity, share the risks and benefits (Siddiqui, 1979: 101-11).

Table: 3.3. An Overview of Comparative Economic Systems

Major Points	Capitalism	Communism and Socialism	Islamic Economy
Property relationship	Man is the owner	State is the owner	Ownership belongs to Allah and the 'man' is a trustee on His behalf
Institutions	Banks, insurance companies and other institutions	Centralised command institutions	Profit and loss sharing, e.g., *Mudarabah*
Value system	Accredited values	Values given by the command leadership	Divine value system as included in Quran
Motivational aspects	Mainly on account of monetary benefits and incentives	Regimentation	Belief in the Hereafter
Production system	No differentiation between *Haram* and *Halal*	No differentiation between *Haram* and *Halal*	Production of *Haram* products is prohibited
Earnings	No difference between *Haram* and *Halal*	No differentiation between *Haram* and *Halal*	*Haram* earnings are prohibited and *Halal* is mandatory

Source: Saeed, 1999: 90.

Note: In Islam, *Haram* means all those items or actions which are prohibited whilst *Halal* means all those that are allowed.

The current global experience indicates that the gulf between rich and poor countries is widening and that the policies of the World Bank and the IMF, whose strategies are purely based on high interest rates while in theory working for the betterment of poor countries, are causing more harm than benefit. One of the most important mechanisms used to assess the debt burden is the calculation of 'debt servicing as a percent of government revenue'. It gives the ratio of the revenue paid to the IMF, the World Bank and other major lenders in relation to what remains in order to fulfil the basic necessities of life needed to keep people alive in debtor countries. It is important to mention here that a major chunk of the budgets of several Muslim countries are allocated for the payment of interest on previous loans.

Under these financial circumstances, it is extremely difficult for developing countries, and Muslim countries in particular, to become competitive in the globalisation process. This situation is further exacerbated by the fact that several Muslim countries are caught in a poverty spiral requiring further loans simply to pay the annual interest instalments of their previous loans (UNDP, 1999, 2000). According to the World Bank's (2000: 228-30) own figures, in 1997, Lebanon paid 93 percent of its revenue for the purpose of debt servicing. How is a country expected to adequately function on only seven percent of its total revenues? Similarly, other Muslim countries such as Turkey, Albania and Pakistan were spending more than one third of their total revenues on debt servicing. This situation is not as serious in Non-Muslim countries as it is in the Muslim World. Overall, the low-income Muslim countries ware paying 21 percent of their revenue to debt servicing as compared to the Non-Muslim countries where the respective figure was 15 percent. Statistics indicate that the World Bank and the IMF are the major financial lenders in both the Muslim and the Non-Muslim worlds, with the United Nations coming third. However, the latter's share in economic matters is significantly less when seen in comparison with the big two. This situation clearly highlights just who is controlling and benefiting from the international financial market.

International Aid

A careful overview of the current global situation shows that international financial aid is provided for four main reasons: i) to further the strategic and political interests of donors, ii) to further the economic, including commercial, interests of donors, iii) in response to humanitarian (ethical and moral) imperatives, and iv) in response to additional or complementary imperatives arising from historical relations between donor and recipient (Riddell, 1996:1). International aid is in fact an important component of the global financial system and is closely associated with the donors' own political interest rather than the real needs of a recipient country. Many examples can be quoted in this regard. One of the most startling is the American threat to the Palestinians that they will withdraw their aid if the latter declare the independent state that is their birthright. This threat was made after the failure of the Camp David Israeli-Palestinian talks sponsored by America. By applying the 'carrot and stick' principle, the United States offered more aid to the Palestinians, reliant on them accepting her formula for agreement between the two parties (*Economist*, 22 and 29 July 2000; *Time*, 7 August 2000). This situation is in stark contrast to the position of Israel who receive the highest per capita aid in the world as a result of American patronage (UNDP, 1999; IISS, 2000).

The following table also reflects a similar situation. Here, low-income Muslim and Non-Muslim categories are compared with regard to the per capita and growth rate of aid given during 1991-97 period. Figures indicate that the Non-Muslim countries were receiving more aid as compared to the Muslim countries. However, the important factor was that during this period, the growth rate of aid to the Muslim World was nearly '-1' as compared to the Non-Muslim countries where the respective figure was '2'. This can possibly be attributed to the attitude of industrial countries in general towards the Muslim World and the role of the global media in associating terrorism with Islam.

Table: 3.4. The Situation of International Aid
to the Muslim and the Non-Muslim Worlds

Category	Aid per capita (US$)	Per year growth rate (1991-97)
Low-income Muslim countries	61.34	-0.91
Low-income Non-Muslim countries	69.82	2.01

Source: Computed from: UNDP, 1999; World Bank, 2000.

Note: These figures represent only those countries for which data was available.

The World Bank (2000) admitted that the levels of aid grants began to fall in the 1990s, just as policy improvements in certain regimes were enabling countries to use aid more effectively. As mentioned earlier, the *New Internationalists Publications* (1999), highlights the political element lying at the heart of international aid: 'So-called development aid is just one aspect of the relationship between poor and rich countries. It is closely linked to the policies of international financial organisations, international trade relationships and, increasingly in recent years, the choices of multinational corporations.' This discussion reflects the strong political factors behind the granting of aid or the advancing of loans. It is also obvious that the Muslim World is under more comparative pressure to repay these loans whilst at the same time ·receiving less financial benefits from the international financial system.

Oxfam is a pivotal institution with regard to the policies of the IMF and the World Bank. In one of its reports, it argues that the

IMF is different from the agency originally envisaged by its chief architect Keynes. According to its first Article, the primary objective of this institution was to promote employment and real income. Similarly, the World Bank was set up to support reconstruction in Europe and to channel resources to developing countries in order to raise the standards of living and conditions of labour. Oxfam argues that the world that the IMF and the World Bank were created to serve no longer exists in spite of the fact that they control billions of dollars in direct and indirect funds (Watkins, 1995:72).

Can we envisage any possible solution to the current state of affairs? In fact, the current struggle and protests of working classes all over the developed world against the policies of these two major global financial institutions should be praised. It is widely believed that the conditionalities imposed on countries in dire financial straits are generally too harsh and if implemented could result in further complicating the financial problems for their governments and creating unrest among their populations. The people living in developing countries feel that all loans and grants given to their countries are primarily based on how good their relations are with the major global players, particularly the United States. For instance, if a country has allowed the United States to use its military bases to direct operations against a neighbouring country or has agreed to play the role of a policeman on its behalf, then it deserves and receives full support, otherwise is branded as corrupt by American ratings agencies or accused of involvement in terrorism or drug trafficking.

The intermittent imposition of unjustified conditions by the IMF and the World Bank cannot be taken to be in the real interests of any country or its people. For instance, increases in water, electricity and gas rates, the imposition of heavy taxes on low-income masses and the increase in petroleum rates, all ultimately affect the prices of all those commodities deemed to be the basic necessities of life. In the case of developed countries such as the United Sates, the petroleum prices, and indeed a number of other commodities, were last revised in the early eighties (*Times*, 23 October 2000).[9]

Another important point of common knowledge that forms one of the basic principles of economics is the fact that the prosperity of a country is not possible unless the savings rate of its people increases and this only occurs when their income exceeds their expenses. Furthermore, it is the responsibility of the government to create such conditions in the country so that people are motivated to convert their savings into investment (Todaro, 1989; Galbraith and Salinger, 1990). The current global system does not offer such opportunities and possibilities for the developing world. It is this lack of investment that is one of the main causes of instability and insecurity. This situation is exacerbated by the fact the financial situation is comparatively more critical and instable in the Muslim World, which in turn adversely effects the low-income Muslim countries. Added to this is the present position and workings of the international financial institutions, which act as a retarding force in the efforts of the developing countries to participate in the globalisation process.

This discussion indicates that the purpose and the function of global finance is to serve the needs of the most powerful countries by allowing them to dictate the terms of involvement to all the others. Unfortunately, in the present global financial system, developing countries, particularly the Muslim countries have no voice.

Notes:

[1] Christian Aid reveals that the chancellor of exchequer is the UK's Governor for both the IMF and the World Bank. The chancellor is accountable to parliament for the money given to these two organisations, but there is almost no opportunity for debate. Contributions to these institutions, which are derived from taxpayers' money, are only discussed once every three years in parliament. Technically, there should be a discussion in the 'foreign affairs select committee', which would allow for a more in-depth debate, but this has never happened. John Denham MP, who is also a member of Christian Aid's Board, wrote to the UK Executive Director asking him for a copy of a World Bank paper which was about to be discussed by the Board of Directors. He was told that the paper was confidential; ironically, the subject of the paper was access to information. Is this a democratic way to keep the British taxpayers informed as to where and how their money is being spent?

[2] Soren Ambrose is a policy analyst and is associated with two Washington based international organisations; 'Alliance for Global Justice' and '50 Years is Enough: US Network for Global Economic Justice. The authors are thankful to Ambrose who through several e-mails, provided useful information for this discussion.

[3] Multilateral debt is that part of a country's external debt burden owed to international financial institutions, particularly the IMF and the World Bank. For most of the world's poorest countries, multilateral debt is larger than other debts because of these institutions' status as 'preferred creditors', and providers of core development and balance of payment loans. This status means that payments to them must be given the highest priority, even over private and bilateral (government-to-government) debt. These institutions also maintain that their bylaws prohibit them from granting substantial debt relief or allowing for the writing off debts. Governments must attend to these multilateral debts as a matter of prime importance, since these both institutions determine the creditworthiness of countries. Until the IMF gives its stamp of approval, which usually requires adherence to the economic policies it recommends, poor countries generally cannot get credit from other sources.

[4] G-8 includes, USA, UK, Canada, France, Germany, Italy, Japan and Russia. These countries are considered the major players in the contemporary globalisation process.

[5] In *Human Development Report 1994*, the UNDP (1994:71) quoted the outcome of a survey on international aid. It stated that: 'Since most people [in the developed world] approve of aid, they do not want their country to be

seen as a "bad donor", giving proportionately less than other countries. They also disapprove strongly of tied aid. A survey in Canada found that 70% of the respondents considered this an immoral and exploitative practice.'

[6] Personal communication with a Kuwaiti professor of Economics (April 2000, UK).

[7] On an overall basis the per capita debt burden of the Muslim world was recorded at US$ 520 as against US$ 364 of the Non-Muslim World (UNDP, 1999 and World Bank, 1999).

[8] See chapter two.

[9] A large number of people argue that in an effort to generate more national revenue, why didn't the World Bank and the IMF advise the industrial countries to enhance the petroleum rates.

4

The Trade Trap
and the Moral Gap

It is a common observation that voices of opposition are being increasingly raised against globalisation. People, particularly from the developing countries, feel that globalisation has primarily resulted in the economic, cultural and ultimately political domination of industrial countries. The democratisation of the market through an expansion of justice, equality and human rights, as well as developing a cultural awareness about ecological issues and conservation, are the minimum first phase benefits expected from the globalisation process. However, in reality what we are in fact witnessing is another form of colonisation or, what might be more accurately termed, 'recolonisation' – a tool of the West to exploit the East in order to expand and maximise the capitalist market through the workings of major international financial organisations such as the IMF and the World Bank.

The World Trade Organisation (WTO) is considered to be one of the most important vehicles of globalisation. This organisation is the successor to the General Agreement on Trade and Tariff (GATT) which pursued, albeit in less aggressive terms, the same objective of promoting larger world trade. The fury of the developing countries and other interest groups affected by WTO policies was clearly visible at Seattle in December 1999. As a result of the large-scale level of protests,

President Clinton in his address to the ministerial meeting voiced sympathies for the concerns of the protesters and advocated an economic order with a humane face (Ahmad, 2000).

WTO – the Third Sister

The state of global finance and the role of major international financial situations have already been discussed in previous chapter. Within the context of this developmental agenda the WTO has emerged as the 'third sister' of these institutions. In financial sectors, the World Bank and the IMF have worked closely together in shaping and reshaping global financial affairs. One of their main areas of concern was how to tackle the problem of non-restrained trade in goods? This issue was the major topic of discussion at two forums; the Project for International Trade Organisation at the UN, and the International Conference on Multilateral Reduction of Barriers on International Trade. These activities resulted in the formation of the General Agreement on Tariffs and Trade (GATT) at Geneva in 1947, followed by the International Trade Organisation (ITO) established at Havana in 1948. However, problems arose when the country, which initiated the process of the ITO refused to ratify the agreement resulting in the organisation being deprived of any power or practical effectiveness. The ensuing gap was breached by the GATT which stepped in to become the main platform for all matters related to international trade through the process of multilateral trade negotiations known as 'Rounds'.

Unlike the World Bank and the IMF, the GATT was not an organisation and so did not possess any members. Instead it had contracting parties which were selected when a state submitted its candidature and negotiated concessions relating to custom duties and access to markets. The objective of the GATT was to conclude agreements on the basis of reciprocity and mutual advantage, based on two fundamental obligations: first each party must accept the notion of the 'most favoured nation' (MNF), meaning concessions accorded by one party to another were generalised to all parties; second, all parities must grant tariff concessions to the other parties.

This type of arrangement suited the industrial countries, especially the USA, at that time and it set a precedent for how GATT was to continue to function over the next four decades. What was misunderstood by the developing counties at the time was the fact that following the abortion of the ITO, the GATT was impregnated with a surrogate fetus which was to be nourished by the 'Rounds' for decades, eventually being born, at a date suitable for the industrial countries, as an addition to the World Bank and IMF family. That date turned out to be the 1st January 1995 and the new institution was named the World Trade Organisation (WTO). Two important 'rounds', the Kennedy Round, which lasted until 1967 and the Tokyo Round, which stretched from 1973 to 1979, have assumed a place of huge significance in the history of GATT. The first worked successfully in decreasing customs duties as well as negotiating for the implementation of anti-dumping practices, while the second concentrated on non-tariff barriers such as technical barriers to trade, government procurement, subsidies, import licensing and anti-dumping practices, all which were subsequently signed into law (Coote and LeQuesne, 1996).

The 1980s saw a change in the global economic environment with countries like the USA finding commodities that they had invented, invading their markets from foreign sources. Most prominent amongst these products were automobile and electrical appliances coming from countries such as Japan, South Korea and China. Moreover, it was also realised that GATT was deficient and unable to legislate for the trade in services, agriculture and dispute settlements. Furthermore, trade-related intellectual property rights were also suffering in the field of patents. This worrying scenario generated two major responses. First, the initiation of a third and final 'round' which was tabled at Geneva in 1982, and served as the basis for the Uruguay Round that was launched at Funta Del Este in 1986. In 1991, a draft of the final act based on a whole series of discussions was eventually presented for approval. However, this draft took another two years to reshape before the differences between the EU and USA were finally resolved on the 15th April 1994. This settlement of differences led to the birth of the WTO on the 1st January 1995, and its subsequent ratification by 127 countries. From then on this surrogate child of GATT became a fully-fledged international organisation with legal status, possessing governing bodies, rights and obligations in close proximity with her sister organisations the IMF and the World Bank. It strengthened the previous agreements on GATT and added new trading systems in agriculture, textiles and investment in service and trade-related property rights.

Secondly, they created regional trading blocs to keep trade within specified spheres. The oldest among them was the European Union (EU), while the youngest, the North America Free Trade Agreement (NAFTA), established in 1994, comprised of the US, Canada and Mexico. This proved to be a very astute move by the USA, knowing that the Uruguay Round was in its final phase and that at its conclusion it (USA) would be able to take advantage of the privileges given to developing countries through the regional trading blocs[1] (Masuel, 1999).

WTO – Another Challenge for the Developing World

According to the World Bank (1999:53): 'The international trading system owes its robust development to successful institutions that straddle international and national levels – for many decades the GATT and now its successor, the WTO. An effective WTO can serve the interests of developing countries in four ways: It can facilitate trade reform, provide mechanisms for settling disputes, strengthen the credibility of trade reforms, and promote transparent trade regimes that lower transaction costs.' The Bank is in fact, the master of creating illusion through statistics – it provided figures that showed that the developing countries share in global trade was increasing faster than at any other previous time in history. The Bank argued that it was due to the beneficial role of these organisations that more developing countries had joined the WTO – in 1987, as many as 65 developing countries were members of GATT while in 1999, there were 110 non-OECD developing countries registered as members of the WTO. The question that then arises is, if this is true, then (as mentioned in chapter one) why has the gap between the developed and the developing worlds continued to increase? The gap between rich and poor is constantly widening. The current situation indicates that the integration of developing countries into the global trading and financial system is not resulting in growth but in increased external deficits and instability (Bashar, 1999). In this context how can the World Bank and IMF possibly seek to justify their policy claims of helping developing countries?

In its report entitled *Trade and Development Report 1999*, the United Nations Conference on Trade and Development (UNCTAD, 2000) reveals that the closer integration of developing countries into the global trading and financial system is not bringing faster growth but leading to increased external deficits and instability. The report argues that in the present era, when the world economy is more integrated than at any other time in its recent history, developing countries depend even more on external resources in order to achieve sufficient rates of growth with which to address the deep-rooted problems of poverty and underdevelopment. The report estimated that in the low-level technology industries alone, developing countries were missing out on an additional US$ 700 billion in annual export earnings. It is important to note that nearly all Muslim countries belong to the group of developing countries, and as a result they are particularly vulnerable to the dangers of this situation because of their crisis-ridden economies, unstable political situation, and low prestige at the international level. Thus, their future prospects in the context of increasing globalised trade appears to be rather bleak unless they manage to shift their focus from internal conflicts to speedy socio-economic development.

The widespread unrest that took place in Seattle was soon followed by equally hostile demonstrations at the World Bank and IMF annual conference in Washington in April 2000. These protests helped to highlight the protesters' main argument; that global free trade is actually widening, instead of closing the gap between the rich and the poor (both within countries and between them). Several other international conferences, including the OECD conference in Bologna (Italy), as well as a number of others held in India and South East Asia during the year 2000, aroused similar opposition with screaming mobs of activists determined to overturn the prevailing unjust international trading and economic order. The question that must then be asked is, in reality who needs the WTO? In one of its issues, the weekly *Economist* (4 December 2000) writes: 'Whether the WTO overcomes this week's setback and becomes a powerful force for good, depends not on the organisation itself [where a large number of developing countries are members] but on governments [of rich nations], especially America. It is they who will decide whether this powerful but anomalous apparatus will be used to advance trade. The outcome can no longer be taken for granted.'

Who is taking Advantage of Global Trade?

According to *The World Guide*: 'Globalisation is really a euphemism for "trans-nationalisation" the unfettered expansion of transnational corporations (TNCs) into the world economy, particularly into the economies of the poor countries. Today TNC have almost total control over the process of globalisation. More than 2/3 of international trade is under the control of a mere 500 corporations. Furthermore, a total of 40% of the trade they control occurs between different parts of the same TNC. Multilateral organisations such as the WTO, IMF and the World Bank are playing a key role in facilitating this process' (New International Publications Ltd. 1999: 63). In a similar context, Jeremy Kahn (2000) reveals that 1999 was a very fruitful year for the worlds top 500 TNCs as their total profit had increased by 26 percent over the past four years.

Table: 4.1. A Snapshot of the Top-500 Companies of the World

Indicator	Amount and numbers	Increase 1998-99 (percent)
Revenue (US$ in billion)	12,696	10.6
Profit (US$ in billion)	554	25.7
Assets (US$ in billion)	44,003	12.9
Employees (number)	43,955,988	10.8

Source: Computed from Jeremy Kahn, 2000.

It is important to know who the owners of these companies are and how many of these companies are owned by Muslim countries. Statistics indicate that of the 500 top companies, 179 were American based, followed by Japan (107), the UK (38), Germany and France (37 each). Similarly, the Unites States, where only 4.6 percent of the global population lives (World Bank, 1999), receives more than 55 percent of the profit from world trade (table: 4.2). The top four companies in the world (i.e., General Motors, Wal-Mart Stores, Exxon Mobil and Ford

Motors) are also American. It is important to note that out of these 500 companies, only one, i.e., Petronas was owned by a Muslim country (Malaysia). In 1999, there were 26 major oil companies out of which nine were American based, seven European and four were of Japanese origin. Developing countries like India and China, which are major importers of oil, also possess major oil companies with multi-million turnovers. Unfortunately, the Middle Eastern Muslim countries, which produce most of world's oil, have no major company to conduct their oil business (Jeremy Kahn, 2000). This situation indicates the poor position of Muslim countries within the global trade market. They are unable to play an active role in the process of globalisation apart from opening their borders and making their trade policy flexible enough for the further expansion of existing corporations in the global market.

Table: 4.2. Rank of Countries with Respect to Owing the Top-500 Companies of the World

Country	Total No. of companies owned	Total revenue US$ in million	Total profit	
			US$ in million	% of total profit
USA	179	4,680,625	308,219	55.54
Japan	107	2,930,835	22,228	3.94
UK	38	764,627	52,463	9.35
Germany	37	1,217,006	31,775	5.75
France	37	922,296	29,270	5.21
Others	102	2,183,712	112,324	20.18

Source: Same as table 4.2.

Note: i) Last Column: % of total profit is the percentage of the profit of a
         respective country's companies with regard to the total profit of all
         500 companies of the world.

         ii) Others: includes Australia, Belgium, Brazil, Canada, China,
         Finland, India, Italy, Luxembourg, Malaysia, Mexico, Netherlands,
         Norway, Russia, South Africa, South Korea, Spain, Sweden,
         Switzerland, and Taiwan.

There is also another way in which to view the contemporary
position of the Muslim World in the global trade market. Table
4.3 indicates the growth rate of trade from low-income Muslim
and the Non-Muslim countries. The figures reflect the fact that
Non-Muslim countries are in a better position as compared to
their Muslim counterparts. During 1980-97, the export growth
of Non-Muslim countries was nearly double that of Muslim
countries. Similarly, in the case of Non-Muslim countries the
growth rate of exports has been higher in comparison to imports.
This situation was reversed in the case of Muslim countries
where the growth rate for imports was higher than that for
exports, reflecting the fact that they had comparatively fewer
opportunities for earning foreign exchange and hard currency
than the Non-Muslim World. The same is also true for the
balance of trade where the figure for Muslim countries was (–)
7.8 as against (–) 4.6 for Non-Muslim countries.

There are at least two main reasons for this sorry state of
international trade in the Muslim World. In the case of oil
producing Muslim countries, the demand for consumer goods
has exceeded the domestic production. So far as the non-oil
producing Muslim countries are concerned, due to their low
agricultural and industrial productivity as well as lack of foreign
investment, their exports have been unable to mach their
imports. Thus in both cases, the balance of trade has always
been negative.

Table: 4.3. Growth Rate of Trade (goods & services) of the Low
Income Muslim and the Non-Muslim Countries

(percentages)

Countries	Export	Import	Balance of trade
Muslim countries	5.65	6.23	-7.83
Non-Muslim countries	10.03	8.26	-4.56

Source: Computed from World Bank, 1999.

Foreign Investment

It should be noted that, a developing country's ability to attract foreign investment mainly depends on international, national and firm-level factors that include international trade policy variables, major currency alignments, and shifts in global corporate strategies, all of which lie beyond the control of the individual government of the host country. In this context, foreign trade becomes closely associated with and linked to foreign investment. It is common knowledge that countries possessing high levels of foreign investment will have increased production resulting in higher exports and greater participation in international trade. Unfortunately, like all other indicators, the Muslim World is also lagging well behind the rest of the world in this field. The following table indicates that in the case of high-income countries, there was nearly 15 times more investment in Non-Muslim countries as compared to Muslim countries. Similarly, in the case of low-income countries, the Muslim countries could only attract one-sixth of foreign investment as compared to Non-Muslim ones. These figures also show that Muslim countries have had to depend on their own limited resources due to the fact that they have been unsuccessful in attracting foreign capital. In the twenty-first century, and with particular reference to the high population growth rate in the Muslim World,[2] this situation does not paint a very healthy picture.

Table: 4.4. State of Foreign Investment in
the Muslim and the Non-Muslim World

Countries	Per capita investment (US$)	Foreign investment as a % of total investment
Muslim World		
• High income countries	29.32	20.23
• Low income countries	12.85	27.27
Non-Muslim World		
• High income countries	432.45	23.20
• Low income countries	72.44	34.44

Source: UNDP, 1999; World Bank, 2000.

In addition to the scarcity of resources, the other major problem facing the Muslim World is the inadequate use of available resources. It is common knowledge that several ruling families in the Muslim World are billionaires monopolising wealth and power. However, this money is either being spent on luxuries or is invested in Western banks and stock markets. Much has already been written in various journals and newspapers in this regard, and in the words of Koreshi (1995): 'Muslim rulers cannot see – not even the writing on the wall.' According to reports in a British newspaper (*Guardian*, 11 August 1999), one Muslim ruler on a trip abroad, took with him nearly 400 people, 200 tons of luggage, and 25 Rolls Royce's and limousines in more than half a dozen jumbo jets. This was in spite of the fact that unemployment was rising and per capita income was declining in his country. The paper goes on to assert that if every system contains the seeds of its own destruction, then this country must surely stand out as a prime example.

Another British journal, *New Internationalists* (May 2000: 29) provided the following example: 'Despite his wealth, Hassanal Bolkiah Muizzaddin Waddaullah, the Sultan and Prime Minister since 1967, is surrounded by gloom. From his father he inherited a personal fortune estimated at $40 billion, which once placed him at the *Fortune* magazine's list of the world's richest people. Recent reports, however, suggest that his treasure has dwindled to $10 billion – peanuts, these days. The question is: where in earth can it all have gone? It's not to easy to blow $ 30 billion, which is roughly equivalent to the entire annual income of all 125 million people living in Bangladesh. Well, a sizeable chunk of it went on the Sultan's palace, a monstrosity that boasts 1,788 rooms and is larger than the Vatican – in a tiny country with just 300,000 inhabitants. When the Sultans daughter turned 18 he bought her an Airbus. ... After the Sultanate's independence from Britain in 1984, they bought 2000 luxury limousines and became the world's biggest customers for Rolls Royce motor cars. ... Such large sums of cash automatically attract political interest. In 1987, it was reported that when US colonel Oliver North asked the Sultanate for help in subverting the Nicaraguan Government – $10 million was duly deposited in a Swiss bank account' Was his excellency also generous for the deprived masses in Afghanistan, Palestine, Kashmir and Somalia?.

Is there a Way-out of this Vicious Circle?

The above discussion suggests that a possible solution for remedying the current position of Muslim countries in the global system would be to adopt a common strategy to promote mutual trade. While highlighting the need for a 'common Islamic market', Kasem Khan (1996: 201-04) emphasised the concept in its historical perspective and in his view: 'An Islamic Common Market is a concept which has a firm basis in Islamic history. The establishment of the Islamic State in Medina founded the first Common Market. The dismantling of tribal, cultural and racial barriers by Islam led to a society based on religious brotherhood which transcended geographical boundaries. This new system was to unleash the entrepreneurial and trading agencies of the Muslims who with the passage of time were determined to establish the greatest economic organisation the world has seen stretching from Morocco to Indonesia. ... There was a tremendous growth of trade and industry in the Islamic World due to three main reasons: i) a vast and diverse geographical area united by common ideology, ii) regional specialisation, and, iii) tariff preferences. The decline of this vast economic organisation began in the 16th century and was due to: i) the opening of new trade routes by European powers in the 16th century, ii) colonisation in the 17th century, and, iii) the impact of the Industrial Revolution in the 17th and 18th century.

This concept was also supported by Sartaj Aziz, former finance and foreign minister of Pakistan (*Dawn*, 26 April 2000), who argued that, compared to the Western industrial countries, the Islamic World had the added advantage of the common ideology of *Ummah*. Unfortunately, due to a lack of proper implementation and planning, these promising proposals and blueprints for economic integration among the Islamic states never got off the ground. However, there are a number of other difficulties that arise in attempting to increase the level of trade among Muslim countries. For instance, Ahsan (1988: 92) pointed out that many of the Muslim countries depend upon a single or at best limited number of commodities for the greater part of their revenue. In addition, there are also some other internal and external problems such as the protectionist policies adopted by major industrial countries, tariff and non-tariff barriers, the impact of debt crisis, lack of infrastructural facilities, close historical relationships with former colonial powers and above all the lack of political will on the part of the Muslim leadership (Shakweer, 1996). However, in spite of these difficulties there is an enormous potential for the development of intra-Islamic trade. Various studies have already been conducted in this regard highlighting many trade avenues in which Muslim countries can cooperate for mutual benefit (Islamic Research and Training Institute, 1992; Ahmed, 1991; Ahmad, 1995; Shalaby, 1988; Cindourki, 1992). For instance:

- The Muslim countries possess significant comparative advantages in labour intensive products.

- In textile, clothing, fibres and yarn, Muslim countries have substantial surpluses and a wide spectrum of complementarities.

- The potential for trade in food and agricultural products is enormous and the same is also true for crude and manufactured items, and pharmaceutical products.

- The potential is also particularly high with respect to the fact that some countries are rich in minerals, others have an abundance of human capital, while some countries have sufficient financial resources to finance any project of mutual interest.

Islamic Economic Union

Regional economic integration organisations like the EU, NAFTA and ASEAN are the main focus of international attention and concern as global economic regionalism increases day-by-day. However, intra-Islamic trade, which constitutes only around 10 percent of total global trade, is falling in comparison to the proportional trade flows that the developing countries and the industrial countries conduct between themselves (Gilani, 1998). As mentioned earlier, the use of protectionism by the Western industrial countries is undermining the Muslim countries' efforts to effectively utilise their comparative advantage. The existence of non-tariff barriers imposed by the developed countries is another major problem for developing countries, and the Muslim World in particular, especially in those areas where they have a comparative advantage, as in the case of agriculture, textiles and light manufacturing (Finger, 1994; UNDP, 1994). In order to overcome such problems and to promote mutual trade within the Muslim World, Muslim countries, like many other countries around the world, have established various regional organisations (Haider, 1994, Bhuyan *et. al.*, 1996, Graff, 1998). For instance:

- Arab Common Market (ACM) 1964
- Central African Customs and Economic Union (CACEU) 1966
- West African Economic Community (WAEC) 1974
- Economic Community of West African States (ECOWAS) 1975
- Economic Cooperation Organisation (ECO) 1985
- Arab Maghreb Union (AMU) 1987
- The Gulf Cooperation Council (GCC) 1987
- The Arab Cooperation Council (ACC) 1989
- Developing Eight (D-8) 1997
- Arab Free Trade Area (AFTA) 1998

Due to the limited activities of most of these economic trade blocs, only the situation of the Economic Cooperation Organisation (ECO) will be discussed here. This organisation comprises of 10 Muslim countries, i.e., Afghanistan, Azerbaijan, Kyrgyzstan, Kazakhstan, Tajikistan, Turkmenistan, Uzbekistan, Pakistan, Iran and Turkey. With a total population of 347 million and covering an area of nearly eight million km^2, the ECO is one of the largest economic unions within the Muslim World. On a collective basis it is rich in oil, gas, cotton and other resources. Six out of the ten ECO member states are land-locked. As air transport is expensive and a direct maritime outlet is not available road and rail links, within and outside the region, assume the utmost importance.

There are vast resources of minerals in these states. Uzbekistan is rich in natural gas. Tajikistan has a huge potential of power generation, while Turkmenistan has large oil and gas reserves. In conjunction with oil and gas, Uzbekistan and Azerbaijan are also producers of cotton and textile products. However, these resources have not been properly exploited and as a result these states still remain greatly underdeveloped. Pakistan, Iran and Turkey were the founding members of the ECO. Turkey with its fast growing economy has closer ties with the Western World. Uzbekistan and Azerbaijan look to Turkey to play a leadership role, while Turkey is unlikely to foster relations based on religion being more interested in spreading the idea of pan-Turkism. In fact, the improvement of ties with the Central Asian states is an important component of Turkish foreign policy. Iran's joint border with Turkmenistan[3] and Azerbaijan, as well as their long-standing cultural and religious relations play an important role in countering the Turkish secular influence. Pakistan was the first country to recognise the independence of all six republics and quickly moved to exchange diplomatic representatives. However, due to the internal turmoil and regional geo-political situation (particularly the civil war in Afghanistan), Pakistan has not been able to effect or achieve very much influence with the new Central Asian Republics (CAR).

It is important for member states to be aware of the fact that in order to improve their integrative efforts in the region, the CAR's should take stock of what they have to offer and what the ECO founding members, i.e., Iran, Pakistan and Turkey, can do to help them. Rather than competing individually, all efforts should be made jointly so that dependency on Western countries is reduced. In spite of the fact that there is immense scope for the enhancement of economic relations, the volatile political situation in Afghanistan and the intermittent but continuing internal crisis in Pakistan, remain real and serious problems. If the conflict in Afghanistan was ended, a direct link could be established between Karachi and the CAR's. At present, this link is impossible, as 600 km's of the necessary territory needed inside Afghanistan is inaccessible because of the continued civil war. This conflict is also holding up the oil pipeline project that could bring the oil of Central Asia to the rest of the world.

There is no doubt that the ECO, as a result of political and economic factors, has thus far failed to take-off. The June 2000 summit held in Tehran, failed to achieve any significant or concrete measures for the future development of the alliance (Masud, 24 June 2000). Although the potential mutuality of economic interests between these countries is obvious, the perceived dissonance of political and security interests, as reflected in the Afghan conflict, remains a major obstacle along the path of regional cooperation. This situation demands that under the current circumstances, the founding members, and Pakistan in particular, should reformulate their foreign policy to make it more compatible with regional and global circumstances. What this means in practical terms is that they should concentrate more on common economic interests than the politics of rivalry. Since the advent of Khatami's presidency in Iran, the Islamic Republic has improved its relationship with the entire region but is continuing to suffer from internal conflicts centred on issues such as development policy and freedom of the press. These developments have the effect of damaging Iran's credibility in the eyes of the international community.

Another important point that needs to be highlighted that in the contemporary situation the immediate integration of the economies of all, or the majority of Muslim countries, does not seem feasible. Thus, an alternative approach needs to be suggested where, instead of going for full economic integration all at once, the Muslim countries should adopt a step-by-step approach towards their common goal. Hence, in the first stage of the programme, economic cooperation should be strengthened. At the second stage, the ECO and GCC should attempt to establish a cooperative link between the two organisations. During the third stage, this cooperation would be expanded to include more organisations (i.e., D-8 and AFTA) that would work together on issues of mutual interest and towards larger integration within the framework of the Muslim World. However, the success of such an undertaking depends upon a collective plan, its proper implementation and above all, the political commitment and goodwill of the leaders of the Muslim World. The experience of the past indicates that achieving cooperation amongst the Muslim leaders is not an easy task. However, the experience of the European Union, where former wartime enemies now cooperate in matters of business and politics, may serve as an example and possible framework for the leaders of the Muslim World on how to work together for mutual benefit. Muslim leaders have to come to the realisation that their religion is like a language, a collective force that governs the lives of their people and which allows them to explore opportunities for their own interests.

Notes:

[1] Mexico is considered a developing country.

[2] See table 2.2.

[3] Turkmenistan is one of the richest countries in the world in terms of its natural resources. Turkmenistan possesses 35 percent of the world's reserves of gas, 12 billion tons of oil (just 30% of the territory of Turkmenistan has so far been explored). Its energy reserves (gas, oil and electricity) lay the basis for the development of its economy. After the USA, Russia and Canada, Turkmenistan is the world's fourth largest producer of natural gas.

5

Defence and Human Security

The implications of defence and development are the main subjects of debate, deliberation and review concerning almost every country in the world. If a large proportion of a nation's budget is diverted from development to the defence sector, it is likely to weaken the national economy in the long run. Ironically, many nations these days are choosing to spend the main part of their financial and physical resources on military training and armaments. It is generally considered that high unemployment, sagging economies, instability and the increased deployment of the military in domestic affairs are the main results of heavy defence spending.

However, despite various negative connotations, positive economic benefits in the areas of growth and development can also accrue from high military spending, although both effects are likely to occur separately and at different points in time. Some of these positive benefits are: i) feeding, clothing and housing to a number of people who would otherwise have to be housed and clothed by the civilian economy, ii) providing education, medical care as well as vocational and technical training, iii) engaging in a variety of public works, and, iv) engaging in scientific and technical research and development that would otherwise have to be performed by civilian personnel. The negative effects of defence spending are, broadly speaking: i) reduced Gross Domestic Product (GDP) and decreased proportionate growth, ii) effects on the balance of payments, as the military expenditure causes the movement of financial resources away from the most dynamic sectors of the economy, iii) defence spending is quite often import intensive thereby further worsening the balance of payments effect by using up scarce foreign exchange or adding to already high external debt.

A thorough examination of the economic implications of defence spending has proved difficult, due mainly to the ambiguity that exists over exactly what issues are at stake. There are three considerations that generally guide the focus of such analysis (Kupochan, 1998).

- In the absence of security threats, a nation would certainly be better off economically by spending nothing on defence. On the other hand, if a country faces a potent threat and is forced to spend on defence needs, it is seen to be at a comparative economic disadvantage. This occurs from the fact a significant percentage of defence spending does not produce future income streams, (only a small proportion of it has any real commercial application). Furthermore, the share of Gross National Product (GNP) devoted to defence would undoubtedly be more economically beneficial if it was diverted and invested in facilities, equipment and research programmes within the commercial sectors of society. The key issue here concerns the extent to which military expenditure deprives the economy of growth producing resources.

- It is generally agreed that anything up to eight percent of GNP is considered to be a moderate level of economic spending. Historical records show that much higher levels of defence spending, i.e., above 15 percent of GNP are likely to have a strong and unambiguously harmful affect on overall national economic performance. States that spend such large percentages of their GNP on defence tend to suffer from high rates of inflation and a considerable diversion of resources from commercial industries.

- The economies of less developed countries respond differently to defence spending than do those of industrialised countries. In less developed countries, where only limited resources are available for developmental projects, high levels of defence expenditure impinge more negatively on economic development as compared to the developed countries.

How Much is the World Spending on Defence?

According to a study conducted by the US Department of State (2000), global military spending was once again on the increase after bottoming out in 1996 as a result of the changed post-Cold War climate. The study found that world military spending rose to US\$ 842 billion in 1997, a two percent increase over the previous year. The report goes on to state that: 'This may represent the beginning of an upturn in the world trend, following a 1995-96 low that had fallen 60 percent from the 1987 peak level. ... The developed countries which had slashed military spending by 54 percent from the Cold War highs in 1988, increased spending in 1997 to US\$ 610 billion.' This study revealed that:

- The defence spending of developing countries has been growing since 1993-94, reaching an historic high of US\$ 232 billion in 1997. Furthermore, their share of the world's total defence spending has risen from 17 to 28 percent in a single decade.

- During the period 1987-97, the South Asian share of total world defence spending rose from 0.9 to 2.0 percent (mainly due to the regional conflict in Kashmir).

- OECD countries have also shown a marked increase in expenditure, jumping from 48 to 62 percent during the 1987-97 period. Similarly, NATO's share went up from 44 to 54 percent.

- United States spending in 1997 made up 33 percent of the world total compared to 27 percent in 1987.

- The world's top 10 military spenders in 1997 were, the United States with US$ 276 billion, followed by China 75, Russia and France US$ 42 each, Japan 41, the UK 35, Germany 33, Italy 23 Saudi Arabia 22 and South Korea with a figure of US$ 15 billion.

- The world arms trade rose sharply in 1997 to US$ 55 billion, a 23 percent increase from 1996. Three importing regions – the Middle East, East Asia and Western Europe – accounted for 80 percent of the total world trade in 1997, while in 1987, their share was under two-thirds. With a figure of US$ 53 billion, the Middle Eastern region was at the top of the list of arms importers (33% of the total global imports of arms). Within this region, Saudi Arabia alone spent US$ 31 billion on arms imports. This figure was in addition to the above mentioned US$ 22 billion which the country spent on its military.

- Similarly, arms exports have also increased, up by 23 percent during the period 1995-97. The top exporter was the United States (58 % of global arms exports) followed by Western Europe (30 %).

- One of the most important measures usually taken as an indicator of the cost of military security is the ratio of military expenditure to population. According to this indicator seven out of the top 10 spenders belonged to the Muslim World. These facts clearly reflect the winners and losers in the world arms business.

Table: 5.1. Per capita Military Expenditures
of the Top-10 Countries of the World

Countries	Per capita military expenditure (US$)
Non-Muslim countries • Israel • Singapore • United States	1,690 1,650 1,030
Muslim countries • Kuwait • Qatar • Brunei • Saudi Arabia • United Arab Emirates • Bahrain • Oman	1,500 .. 1,220 1,050 1,020 880 790

Source: Derived from: U.S. Department of State, 2000.

Note: Figure for Qatar was not available in the original source.

As mentioned above, certain countries are shown to allocate a large proportion of their national resources to defence – a fact particularly true of Middle Eastern Muslim Countries. This begs the question as to why these countries, and Muslim countries in particular, spend so much on defence? In this context it is appropriate to draw a comparison between the defence expenditures of the Muslim and the Non-Muslim worlds. Table 5.2 indicates that on an aggregate basis, it is in fact, the Non-Muslim World that is spending more money on defence as compared to the Muslim World. Under present global political circumstances the Muslim World has little hope of curtailing its current defence expenditures. The statistics indicate that with respect to the per capita defence expenditure in the Non-Muslim World both high and low income countries were spending slightly less than double the amount of the high and low income Muslim countries.

In general, the ratio of military expenditure per member of the armed forces is considered as a crude measure of the level of military technology in a country. This ratio was far higher in the Non-Muslim than the Muslim World. Both, high and low income Non-Muslim countries were spending more than double the amount of money of their Muslim comparatives. However, the proportion of armed forces members with respect to population was marginally higher in the Muslim World as compared to the Non-Muslim World. The proportionately higher number of soldiers and the comparatively lower levels of defence expenditure in the Muslim World tend to reflect the low quality of their armed forces in general, and the fact they operate in an environment where they are totally dependent on the import of defence equipment from the West. If Muslim countries could unite like European Union where there was cooperation in political, economic and cultural matters, would they need to spend so much money on defence?

Table: 5.2. Comparison of the Defence Expenditure
and Military Strength with Respect to
Population in the Muslim and
the Non-Muslim Worlds

Item	Muslim World		Non-Muslim World	
	High income countries	Low income countries	High income countries	Low income countries
Per capita defence expenditure (US$)	354	30	592	53
Defence expd. per soldier (US$)	37,316	7140	137,586	16,556
No. of soldier as a % of population	0.95	0.43	0.43	0.32

Source: Computed from IISS, 1999: 300-04.

Uni-Polar World

As was emphasised elsewhere, the United States, following the demise of Soviet Union, now stands alone as the world's only super power. This situation has provided the country with many advantages, particularly in the economic and political arenas. Numerous examples can be quoted here, but this discussion is limited to a few quotations from a single issue of the London based weekly *Economist* (2 September 2000: 58, 65, 82, 101):

- Who could have guessed it? America is into the tenth year of the longest economic boom in its history. The economy is minting millionaires so fast that psychologists have discovered a whole new mental disorder – that results from having huge piles of cash dumped on your head.

- With regard to the Lockerbie trial of two Libyans suspected of blowing up a Pan-Am airliner in 1988...the United Nations released the text of a letter that secretary-general, Kofi Annan, had written to the Libyans in 1999, giving assurances that the trail 'would not be used to undermine the Libyan regime'.

- America has already imposed sanctions on Sudan, accusing it of supporting terrorism.

- [In East Timor] one of the first things it must choose is a currency. Many returned exiles have advocated the Portuguese escudo, and by extension the euro, in recognition of East Timor's colonial links to Portugal. The UN and the World Bank are pushing for the American dollar.

This situation raises a number of serious and pertinent questions. How was it possible for the United States to accumulate such huge global wealth overnight? According to their individual charters, both the United Nations and the World Bank are neutral institutions; why then are they pushing East Timor to adopt the American dollar as its currency? The Western World, and the United States in particular, proved very eager to solve the problem of East Timor. Why then are they not taking the same interest in attempting to solve the problem of Kashmir, in spite of the fact that its population and area is much larger than that of East Timor and that this conflict is affecting nearly a quarter of the global population? Moreover, as the United Nations had no obvious role in bringing the Lockerbie suspects to justice,[1] how then can it provide assurances about the safety of the Libyan regime? Which international law or moral value gives sole authority to the United States to label certain countries as either 'peace loving nations' or 'terrorist states'? It is worth-noting here that even American citizens are not happy with the global bullying of their government. In a letter to the editor of

Economist (2 September 2000: 6), one American citizen writes: 'Sir – You say that western nations imposed sanctions on Sudan for its ill-treatment of its own people and its neighbours ('Sudanese contradictions', August 19th) [2000] but that its government's intentions towards the West may have changed. You also mentioned that oil deposits have been discovered in Sudan. Sudan's attitude has not changed. The only thing that has changed is that there is oil in Sudan and we (Americans) do not yet have a piece of the pie. Michael Del Toro, New York.'

According to the American report discussed earlier, this country is the biggest producer and exporter of arms. A UK based organisation, the International Institute for Strategic Studies, reveals in its report entitled *The Military Balance 1999-2000* (1999) that from 1992-98 the United States was responsible for 44-55 percent of the total arms exported to the rest of the world. Israel, France, Britain, Germany, Italy, China and Russia supplied the remaining 35-45 percent of world arms. Those who supplied only 0-1 percent (US$ 10-50m in total) of total world arms, consisted of a group of 16 countries (table: 5.3).

Therefore, on an average basis, while the United States earned over US$ 20 billion from arms sales, the average individual share of these 16 countries amounted to not more than two million dollars.[2] The report also reveals that the three groups of minor arms exporters, with a combined share of 0-4 percent of the total global arms export market, consisted of 34 countries out of which only 11 belong to the Muslim World. This clearly identifies those countries that are promoting international conflicts and instability through monopolising the global arms market in a bid to sell their arms for maximum profit.

Table: 5.3. Country Suppliers to the International Arms Trade
(1992-98)

US$ 10m - 50m (0-1%)	US$ 50m - 100m (1-2%)	US$ 100m - 200m (2-4%)	US$ 200m - 1 bn (5-10%)	US$ 1 bn – 20 bn (35-45%)	US$ 20 bn+ (45-55%)
Chile	Australia	Argentina	Belarus	China	United
Denmark	India	Austria	Belgium	France	States
Egypt	Iran	Brazil	Canada	Germany	
Finland	Norway	Bulgaria	Czech Rep.	Israel	
Greece	Poland	FRY	Netherlands	Italy	
Hungary	Romania	Indonesia	North	Russia	
Japan	Singapore	Portugal	Korea	UK	
Jordan	Slovakia	South	Spain		
Kazakhstan	Turkey	Korea	South		
Kyrgyzstan	Zimbabwe		Africa		
Malaysia			Sweden		
Mexico			Switzerland		
Pakistan			Ukraine		
Saudi					
Arabia					
Taiwan					
Uzbekistan					

Source: IISS, 1999: 281.

According to Sontag (25 November 1999) and Hunter (1999), the United States and the United Kingdom have no problem with countries developing weapons of mass destruction, as long as they are deemed 'friendly nations'. This was the reason and explanation as to why Israel was not only allowed to develop its own nuclear programme but was also provided with Western assistance in doing so. Similarly, Miller (20 October 1999), Norris, Arkin and Burr (1999) revealed that the United States had stored 12,000 nuclear weapons and their components in 23 countries and five American territories during the Cold War. With regard to Anglo-American foreign policy, Aburish

(1998:48) argued that: 'The division of friendly and non-friendly governments have little to do with their true nature. Historically, legitimate nationalist regimes were rejected when they were considered a threat to Western interests while friendly illegitimate ones were supported regardless.' This is possibly one reason as to why the major global players need to produce arms on such a large scale for export throughout the world.

An Overview of the Arab-Israel Arms Situation

According to the IISS (1999), the Middle East and North African region continues to be the world's largest leading arms market, both in absolute terms and as a proportion of GDP (7%). In 1998, regional military expenditure increased by about seven percent in real terms.[3] In the case of Israel, its 1999 defence budget (US$ 6.8b) showed a marked increase from the previous year in spite of the fact that a significant part of its defence expenditure is received in the form of US Foreign Military Assistance (FMA) which is not counted in the budgetary figures. The same is also true for US Foreign Military Financing (FMF). In the year 2000, the FMF rose from US$ 1.8 billion to 1.9 billion for the procurement of various items for military use.

Under the October 1998 'Why Memorandum', which covered the period 1999-01, Israel was also to receive an additional US$ 1.2 billion in FMA from the United States. Moreover, the initial deployment of the joint US-Israel *Arrow* Anti-Ballistic Missile (ABM) was also planned during 1999-00. In 1998, the Israeli Air Force received the first four of 25 F-15I aircraft, equipped with US advanced air-to-air missiles (AAM) as well as new Israeli *Python*-4 AAM, under a contract worth US$ 2.2 billion for ten years. Its Air Force also ordered a further fifty F-16s from the United States. In March 1999, the Navy of this tiny country received three *Dolphin*-class submarines from Germany as part of a bilateral FMA programme. According to IISS sources, each submarine is estimated to cost US$ 300 million, the financing of which sees Germany contributing US$ 750 million towards the total cost. On the export side, Israel remains one of the top five exporters in the international arms trade (IISS, 1999: 119-22).

How strong is the Arab World by comparison, particularly those four countries that share their borders with Israel? In 1999, the Syrian defence budget was US$ 1.5 billion in total, and it lacked the luxury of any FMA or FMF. In fact, Syrian defence procurements have declined during the 1990s as a result of a dispute over ex-Soviet debts of around US$ 11 billion. Lebanon, which has suffered heavy military and territorial (the so called security zone) losses at the hands of Israel, had a total defence budget of only US$ 560 million in 1999. Jordan's defence budget was even less than Lebanon's (US$ 447m) and it received only US$ 170 million in FMF as against the almost two billion dollars received by Israel. In the financial year 1998-99, the Egyptian defence budget stood at US$ 2.1 billion with the country receiving FMF worth 1.3 billion dollars (IISS, 1999). It is important to mention here that the US-FMF received by Jordan and Egypt was only given as a result of the peace agreement that these countries had made, under the close supervision of the United States, with Israel.

Table 5.4 indicates the level of Israel's military superiority over its four neighbours. The defence budget of this tiny state was significantly higher than the combined defence budgets of all four Arab countries. This is in spite of the fact that the population of this country is nearly 14 times less than its four Arab neighbours. In addition, Israel was also receiving a huge level of military assistance from the United States (520 dollars per capita, as against Egypt and Jordan, where the respective figures were only 21 and 34 dollars per capita). This highlights not only the quantitative but also the qualitative superiority that Israel enjoys over its neighbours.

The above situation can be judged from the fact that Israel was spending US$ 56,686 per soldier as compared to the combined expenditure of US$ 6,541 per soldier of all four Arab countries. This puts the Israeli expenditure at a level nearly nine times higher than that of the Arabs. This superiority is further increased by the fact that it is widely believed that Israel has more than 100 nuclear warheads as well as long range Ballistic and Cruise missiles capable of dispatching them to their desired target (IISS, 1999). Once again, it needs to be highlighted that it is not the Middle Eastern Muslim countries that are promoting the arms race or receiving huge military assistance from the 'global super power'.

It is important to note that as long as United States foreign policy favours Israel, the Arab masses will see this country as hostile to the Arab World. This situation questions the credibility of the United States as a fair and neutral peace broker in the Middle East. It is not just the Arab World that views United States foreign policy as lacking neutrality, non-Arab Muslim countries also see this global super power's foreign policy as biased and unjust in resolving the Middle East crises. Furthermore, apart from the problem of Middle East, the comparative analysis of the situation of Kashmir and East Timor, Somalia, Iraq, Sudan (see chapter 6) and the nuclear issue also reflects the inadequate role of the United States in global affairs. Current global circumstances demand that the activities of the United Nations be strengthened and this organisation be provided every opportunity to lead peace initiatives in war-torn regions. The permanent members of the UN Security Council particularly the Unites States should also realise this fact.[4]

Table: 5.4. A Comparison of the Military Power of Israel
vs Egypt, Jordan, Syria and Lebanon

Item	Israel	Egypt	Jordan	Syria	Lebanon
Total defence Budget (US$m)	6,800	2,100	447	1,500	560
Per capita defence budget (US$)	1,133	34	89	100	140
US-FMA (US$m)	1,200	..	..	..	..
Per capita US-FMA (US$)	200	..	..	..	..
US FMF (US$m)	1,920	1,300	170	..	-
Per capita US FMF (US$)	320	21	34	..	..
Armed forces (000)	175	450	104	320	55
Military spending per soldier (US$)	56,686	7,555	5,933	4,687	10,182
Nuclear Warheads	100+	..	..	..	..
Ballistic & Cruise missiles	*Jericho* 1 (500km) *Jericho* 2 (1,500km) *Delilah*-2 (400km) *Gabriel* 4LR (200km)	Project-T (450km)	..	..	..

Source: Derived form: IISS, 1999: 119-47, 310-12; Thomas, Barry and Liu,
1998: 25 May 1998: 16-21.

Nuclear Issue and the Muslim World

The nuclear issue is a matter of great concern for the whole
world. According to *Time* magazine, by the end of the twentieth
century, the United States was responsible for conducting the
highest number of nuclear tests (1030), followed by USSR
(715), France (210), Britain and China (45 each), India (3) and

Pakistan (2). Effendi (1999) rightly points out that: 'It was an evil day when the US dropped two nuclear bombs on Hiroshima and Nagasaki on the 6th and 8th of August 1945. Hundreds and thousands died on that fateful day. Whatever the strategic reason that motivated the momentous decision to drop these bombs, the US scientific community which developed the weapons of mass destruction were shocked at the enormity of this crime against humanity.' However, this shock did not stop the American government from threatening non-nuclear states with the use of nuclear weapons. According to Schaeffer (1999: 218-19), 'the US has issued nuclear threats on some 20 occasions since it destroyed Hiroshima and Nagasaki... the US has been guilty of only threatening non-nuclear opponents.' This situation has encouraged non-nuclear countries to acquire nuclear technology, resulting in increased regional and global insecurity and tension.

After the demise of the Soviet Union, the West, and in particular the US, saw Islam as the next new global enemy. It then began to instigate a programme that aimed to eliminate and remove Islam from having any active role in global affairs. In 1995, Koreshi[5] wrote that: 'Only a few Muslim countries have the elements of power that can make them either singularly or jointly a powerful group capable of safeguarding their interests in the long run. Among such nations are Egypt, Iraq, Algeria, Iran, Indonesia, and Pakistan. This does not mean that they will become a challenge to the West, but after graduating from a third-class power to a relatively higher status, they can manage their own national interests. To foreclose this possibility, the West is scheming to fix Muslim countries, including even its surrogates and allies, into an iron frame which will reduce their armed forces to local militias rather than modern armies, thus leaving them unable to defend their militarily interests in their own region. This exercise is four-pronged:

- Imposing a technology blockade, to deny them self-reliance in arms production and economic development.

- Chaining them to debilitating regimes through arms control and the denial of hi-tech weapons such as missiles, modern aircraft and equipment. This aims at confining them to low-level defence capabilities while Israel lying to the West and India lying to the East of the targeted areas continue to retain their arms superiority over Muslims.

- Denying them nuclear, laser, and space sciences for defence utilisation purposes. Industrially, they must stay backward so that they remain consumer societies and a large outlet for Western products.

- Eliminating 'Islamism' by changing the basis of Muslim rational identity as a factor in relations between Muslim nations. This is done by preventing them from supporting Muslim movements, and bringing to an end the 'transnationalism of Islam' or the sense of being part of the *Ummah.*'

Koreshi's views are also supported by Judith Miller (19 September 2000), an American writer, who argued: 'The United States has been pressing Russia not to proceed with plans to sell Iran laser technology that Washington says can be used to make fuel for nuclear weapons, according to administration officials. Officials said that since July, President Clinton has raised the prospective sale of laser technology at least twice in meetings with President Vladimir V. Putin. ... The United States has been working for three months to dissuade Russia from letting a centre associated with the D.V. Efremove Institute of St. Petersburg, part of the Atomic Energy Ministry, from proceeding with a contract to sell the technology to Iran.' This discussion reflects that America's nuclear non-proliferation policy can be mathematically expressed as follows (Koreshi, 1995:148):

Permitted Nuclear Powers = {(five major powers) + (Israel) + (India)} − (all Muslim countries)

US' Vision of Nuclear Club in Relation to the Muslim World

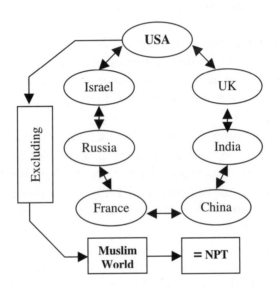

Such an assertion can be posited as one of the reasons as to why the major global players have never been seriously concerned about Indian and Israeli nuclear ambitions. This situation has encouraged both countries to proceed with their nuclear plans and in May 1974, India exploded a nuclear device under the euphemism of a 'peaceful nuclear explosion'. On the 11th of May 1998, India not only conducted a series of nuclear explosions, but followed them up with demands to make her a permanent member of the UN Security Council, whilst at the same threatening Pakistan with military action' (Ali, 1999:26). On the 28th of May, Pakistan conducted its own series of explosions. Following these tests the international community formally condemned both countries and economic sanctions were imposed against them, with the main pressure being put on Pakistan to sign up to the CTBT and NPT. At the time of these tests, the US stated that India had lost forever her justification for a permanent seat on the Security Council. However, two year later the US reversed its decision by stating that it supported India's case for a permanent seat in the Security Council. Immediately after the US statement, the UK, France, Germany and Russia, all issued similar declarations of support (*Dawn*, 11, 13, 17, 19 April 2000).

Indeed, when India conducted its first nuclear test in 1974, the response from the US was lukewarm. Although, Pakistan was subjected to much greater international pressure from the very beginning of its nuclear programme, it did enjoy almost a decade of non-interference with which to develop nuclear warheads as a result of the Russian invasion of Afghanistan. During this period, the US turned a blind eye to Pakistan's nuclear weapons project. In 1989, with the withdrawal of Russian forces form Afghanistan, Pakistan's nuclear potential became a major issue of international concern. Later, with the collapse of the Soviet Union and the ending of the Cold War, another substantial change in US policy towards Pakistan occurred and the discriminatory, controversial and country specific Pressler Amendment was applied solely to Pakistan, quickly followed by the imposition of sanctions (Pamela Newburg, 1994).

This situation indicates the discriminatory and expedient roles played by the West and the US in particular. In early 2000, a report prepared by an American commission and approved by the White House made the following important points (*Akhbar-e-Watan*, March 2000):

- The next 25 years will be disastrous for Paksitan and the security of this country will be in great danger, particularly as a result of the situation in Afghanistan.

- The Taliban may fight against India.

- Paksitan will fight with India over Kashmir.

- Paksitan can be disintegrated by the end of the first quarter of the twenty-first century.

- This situation could lead to war between Iran and India in order to attain a maximum share of the disintegrated Pakistani territory.

This report emerged at a time when American President Bill Clinton was due to visit Pakistan as part of a South Asian tour in April 2000. The question emerges as to what information and factors exist that lead America to conclude that this particular Islamic country will disintegrate within a specific period of time? Are they secretly working on bringing this situation to pass?

There is no doubt that being such an active country in the Muslim World, Pakistan's nuclear programme is a matter of great concern for the United States. On the other hand Israel, which also possesses the required technology and skills to conduct its own nuclear programme and has always refused to sign the NPT, is totally ignored by Western countries. New photographs of the top secret Israeli reactor at Dimona, recently published on internet, confirm that Israel could, according to the Federation of American Scientists (FAS)[6], have produced between 100 and 200 nuclear weapons. The high-resolution pictures, taken in July 2000 by the Space Imaging Corporation's Ikonos satellite showed enough information in order to be able to assess the amount of plutonium that the reactor could produce. It was from these assessments that the size of Israel's weapons stockpile was then calculated. The FAS stated that: 'Based on plausible upper and lower bounds of operating practice at the reactor, Israel could have produced enough plutonium for at least 100 nuclear weapons, but probably not significantly more than 200 weapons' It further reveals that the pictures support claims that Israel could be using highly enriched uranium to build nuclear weapons or to increase the yield of plutonium weapons (FAS, 2000).

According to Avner Cohen (2000),[7] a famous Israeli intellectual; both the United States and France have played an important role in making Israel a nuclear power by turning a blind-eye to its nuclear activities. With regard to the larger international arena, it was Washington's response that would ultimately determine how the international community accepted a nuclear-armed Israel. Israel did not provoke the Arabs into developing their own nuclear weapons or launching an attack on its Dimona reactor. However, when Iraq started its own nuclear programme, Israel responded in 1981 by destroying the Iraqi reactor, demonstrating its determination to deny nuclear weapons to Arabs. The Arab reaction was milder than might have been anticipated. This situation highlights the fact that Israel's nuclear status has contributed greatly to its image as the strongest nation in the Middle East.

Does Israel also possess the capability to deliver these nuclear weapons to their designated targets? Indeed, acquiring the necessary knowledge and facilities with which to be able to dispatch the nuclear weapons to their correct targets is even more important than the nuclear weapons themselves. Israel currently possesses all the necessary facilities in this regard. In addition, with US assistance, this tiny country has also developed anti-missiles, missile-sparrows, and the space vehicle Ofeq-1, which is used for spying, radar jamming, and command and control functions. Furthermore, 'on April 11, 1994, the US

Department of Defence informed Congress that it will sell Israel a fleet of F-15-I planes worth US\$ 2.4 billion. The F-15-I version has a combat range of 2000 miles. A report from Washington points out that refuelled in the air, these planes can bomb Pakistani nuclear installations... Admiral Inmam, a former CIA member disclosed that in 1980, Israel was supplied with satellite photos of Libya and Pakistan, of the same type that were furnished to it in 1980 for the attack on the Iraqi nuclear plant. This revelation confirms the *Washington Post* stories that strikes on Kahuta [Pakistan's nuclear installation] were being planned at this time' (Koreshi, 1995: 154-55). These facts are also confirmed in a report from the IISS (1999:135) which states that: 'Israel is widely believed to have a nuclear capability with up to 100 warheads. Delivery means could include *Jericho*-1 SSM (range up to 500 km) and *Jericho* 2 (range 1500-2000 km).'

Human Security

Human security is generally considered to be a modern concept. In one of its reports, the UNDP (1994:3) argued that: 'For too long, the concept of security has been shaped by the potential for conflict between states. For too long, security has been equated with the threats to a country's borders. For too long, nations have sought arms to protect their security. For most people today, a feeling of insecurity arises more from worries about daily life than from the dread of a cataclysmic world event. Job security, income security, health security, environmental security, security from crimes – these are the emerging concerns of human security all over the world.'

The current global situation shows that the UNDP is only partially right in its arguments. While presenting this new concept, perhaps it has forgotten the widespread persistence of international conflicts all over the world. Even the major global players, which face no obvious threat to their national security, are spending a huge amount of money on military expenditure and defence. This situation leads other countries to follow suit, promoting further conflict and global insecurity. It needs to be emphasised that at the dawn of the twenty-first century, when the United States is considered the only supreme power in the world, how anyone could possibly conceive that a country from the Third World would have the courage or ability to seriously threaten American national security?

Another important fact is that 'human security' is also closely linked with the external security of a country, an issue particularly pertinent in the case of developing and Muslim countries. How can the tens of million of people living in South Asia and the Middle East afford to ignore the issue of external security and concentrate solely on their 'human security'? How is it possible for a weaker country to forget its declared rights and keep itself in a victimised state as a result of aggression from a powerful neighbour? How can a country continue to endure the misery of economic sanctions, imposed on it by international organisations as a result of the influential role of global feudal lords, which are causing the deaths of tens of thousands of innocent children? The UNDP (1994: 8, 84-85) for its part proposes: i) a three percent yearly cut in the defence budgets of all nations, ii) the establishment of an Economic Security Council, and, iii) the establishment of a World Central Bank. It remains to be seen whether the Western industrial countries will take the lead in implementing these recommendations. Furthermore, unlike the UN Security Council and the World Bank, would the proposed Economic Security Council and the World Central Bank function as impartial bodies? In fact, under current global circumstances it seems that the UNDP's views are merely good intentions rather than concrete proposals.

The objective of this discussion is not to justify the maximisation of military expenditure, but to simply make the point that for the Third World in general and the Muslim World in particular, it is not realistic to call for significant defence budget cuts until major international disputes are settled peacefully. The following indicates that among the four groups of countries being examined; the high-income Muslim countries, the majority of which are situated in the Middle Eastern region, were spending the highest proportion of their GDPs (6.7 %) on military and the lowest proportion on education and health. The same was also true for the Muslim World as a whole. In fact, this situation is mainly due to the increased incidence of conflicts and relative instability of the Muslim World. It also reflects the fact that the Muslim World is bearing more of the burden for defence expenditure as compared to the Non-Muslim World. This meant that there were few resources left for expenditure on amenities such as education and health and this is generally seen as one of the main reasons as to why the Muslim World is generally lagging behind the rest of the world in terms of human development.[8]

Table: 5.5. A Comparison of Expenditure on
Education, Health and Military

Country	Education (% of GNP)	Health (% of GDP)	Military (% of GDP)
Muslim World			
• High-income countries	3.4	1.5	6.7
• Low-income countries	4.2	1.8	3.4
Non-Muslim World			
• High-income countries	5.3	6.1	1.7
• Low-income countries	4.4	3.1	2.1

Source: Computed from UNDP, 1990: 162-63; UNDP, 1999: 188-91.

Notes:

[1] With regard to the trial of two Libyan suspects, in late 1999, it was only the American and British governments that gave Qaddafi the ultimatum to - 'take it or leave it'

[2] Around 1000 times less than the United States.

[3] The figures were, US$ 57 billion in 1997 and US$ 61 billion in 1998.

[4] The permanent members of the UN Security Council particularly the United States should realise that with regard to the promotion of their own national interests, undue attempts to influence the UN decision making process and especially the use of veto in the Security Council in favour of Israel will neither help in achieving long-lasting peace, nor will it strengthen the efforts to curb global terrorism. Therefore, they have to understand the root of the problem.

[5] An intellectual, ex-diplomat and liberal Muslim thinker.

[6] FAS is a Washington-based organisation which lobbies on scientific issues and includes 51 Nobel Laureates among its sponsors.

[7] Avner Cohen is a Senior Research Fellow at the National Security Archive, George Washington University.

[8] See chapter two.

6

Western Fundamentalism and Global Politics

Much hue and cry has been made about the perceived threat of 'Islamic Fundamentalism' all over the world. This situation is exaggerated to such an extent that universal facts have been ignored and suppressed in what has amounted to a new undeclared 'Cold War'. It is also common knowledge that this situation has resulted in paralysing the United Nations on many occasions. For this reason, many developing countries consider the development of their role and representation in the UN as the only means of making this world body more democratic and effective. In fact, the present situation of the UN Security Council does not allow for true reforms, as changes are only possible if two-thirds of the members of the organisation, including the permanent members of the Security Council, support the move (*New Internationalist Publications Ltd.*, 1999: 78). Therefore, due to this skewed situation, most of the developing countries, and the Muslim countries in particular, have no real say in global affairs or in the decisions that affect their legitimate rights. This chapter focuses on only five case studies (i.e., Kashmir, Palestine, Somalia, Iraq and Sudan) where it has been shown that the international problems and disputes relating to the Muslim World have been deliberately ignored due to the fact that their resolution was deemed not to be in the interests of the major global players or their allies.

Kashmir and East Timor – When Religion Makes the Difference

The State of Jammu and Kashmir is situated in the extreme North of India and Pakistan and is located in the heart of Central Asia. Apart from the predominantly Muslim district of Gurdaspur, which was deceitfully taken from Pakistan and ceded to India, this state has no common border with India. The State's common frontier with Pakistan is more than 1100 km long and its language is the same as that spoken in Pakistan. According to the census figures of 1941, the overall Muslim population in the State was 80 percent with the remaining 20 percent being comprised mainly of Hindus and Buddhists (Khaliq, 1973:54). At the time of partition (1947), it was decided, on the basis of principle, that all princely states were free to join either India or Pakistan in accordance with their geographical positions and communal complexity. The then Viceroy of India, Lord Mountbatten referred to this principle in his famous address to the organisation of princely states, the Indian Chamber of Princes, on the 25th July of 1947, by stating: 'The States are theoretically free to link their future with whichever dominion they may care. But when I say that they are at liberty to link up with either of the Dominions, may I point out that there are certain geographical compulsions which cannot be evaded. You cannot run away from the Dominion Government which is your neighbour any more than you can run away from the subjects for whose welfare you are responsible' (*Impact International*, 2000:6).

It is beyond the scope of this brief section to present a detailed historical analysis of the Kashmir dispute, except to make the point that in spite of these declarations of facts and principles, Indian forces occupied the State in October 1947 stating that the Dogra Raja of the State of Kashmir had decided to join India. This was the starting point of the dispute between Pakistan and

India (Lamb, 1997; Lamb, 1994; Lamb, 1991; Baker, 1994). In December 1947, India took the matter to the UN Security Council, urging that a world body should take action under article 35 of the United Nations' Charter to solve the issue (Sibtain, 1993). It was the over enthusiastic Lord Mountbatten who assured the Indians that a verdict against Pakistan and in favour of India would be forthcoming sooner than expected (Aziz, 1998). The UN Security Council debated the issue and came to the conclusion that the case was not as India was presenting it but more an unfinished issue related to the freedom of the subcontinent. The Security Council decided that a plebiscite should be held to determine the national affiliations and future course of the State of Jammu and Kashmir. This plebiscite was to be held under the aegis of the United Nations. It is important to note that from 1948 to 1971, nearly one and a half dozen Security Council resolutions have been passed in a bid to resolve the impasse. However, India has been unwilling to implement any of these resolutions, in much the same way that Israel has never accepted UN resolutions with regard to solving Palestine problem.[1]

What prevented the holding of the plebiscite was India's refusal to acknowledge the UN resolutions as well as the lack of commitment on the part of UN itself to implement its own resolutions. The Indian occupation of this State, based solely on its superior military power, has encountered massive resistance from the vast majority of the population. This resistance, which emerged as a result of the failure of the UN resolutions, is now labelled as terrorist actions similar to the way in which Palestinians who demanded their own home-land were labelled terrorists by the Western media. It is important to note that in March 2000, President Clinton, during his visit to South Asia, called Kashmiri freedom-fighters terrorists, thereby ignoring the history of his own country's birth. Were not the American freedom fighters branded rebels and terrorists by the then ruling British government? If we pay heed to his argument in relation to the Kashmiri people's struggle, (who after all are simply fighting for their right to self-determination), then we have to withdraw recognition of the United States government, which was born out of the very same fight for freedom. In this context should American heroes such as Thomas Jefferson, George Washington, Patrick Henry, Benjamin Franklin, Thomas Paine and several others, be called freedom fighters or simply terrorists? To develop the point even further it was US President Teddy Roosevelt, who in March 1903, uttered the following threatening worlds to the Anglo-American Convention, which was then dealing with the Alaska-Canada border issue: 'That which we [Americans] cannot obtain by peace, we will obtain by war' (Tellis, 10 April 2000).

The obvious outcome of a situation of continued oppression and long-standing dispute is the birth of militancy and Kashmir is no different in this respect. The massive deployment by India of a 700,000 strong armed force to suppress the freedom movement has resulted in the deaths of 96,000 Kashmiri men, women and children, 124,500 people being disabled, a further 115,000 been arrested, jailed and tortured, as well as the rape of more than 48,000 women. Thousand are missing and many more have been rendered homeless. Thousands of houses including a number of holy shrines have been burnt and destroyed (Rafi and Karipak (eds.), 1990; Human Rights Watch, 1991 and 1996, Jan, 1991; Amin, 1995; Kamal, 1996; Salahddeen, 19 August 1997; Haq, 15 April 2000; Sayeed, 31 May 2000;). Who is responsible for this continued violation of basic human rights?

With regard to contextual reference, it is imperative to review the situation of Kashmir in relation to East Timor. The review of these two cases reflects the double standards operated by the major global players which dominate the United Nations. Following the UN supervised referendum of 1999, East Timor is now an independent country. The people of East Timor were allowed the right of self-determination – a principle that the

United Nations has ignored in the case of Kashmir. East Timor was a Portuguese colonial outpost until 1974. The outbreak of civil war lead to Indonesian military intervention that finally ended with its annexation to Indonesia. Due to the widespread unrest and civil war, the UN and the Western countries refused to recognise this annexation. In December 1975, the Security Council passed Resolution 384 that recognised the 'inalienable right of the people of East Timor to self-determination and independence in accordance with the principle of the Charter of the United Nations' and called upon Indonesia to withdraw its forces from the territory (Article 2). In 1976, Resolution 389 of the Security Council once again reaffirmed this position (Mirza, 2000:110-11). It is worth noting that within less than a quarter of a century the East Timorese have been granted the right of self-determination, a right that has been continually denied to Kashmiris for more than half a century.

This situation raises the question, on the basis of principle, whether the case of East Timor is somehow stronger and more clear-cut than that of Kashmir? The answer is most certainly 'no' as table 6.1 highlights. It is widely believed in the Muslim World that when Muslims are suffering in the hands of non-Muslims (e.g., Palestine and Kashmir), the international community is not serious in the provision of basic human and birth-rights to the Muslim masses. However, in contrast, if they (i.e., western industrial countries) believe that the non-Muslim is oppressed by Muslims (e.g., East Timor), they will take prompt and strict action supported by their military power, global media, international politics and international financial institutions. This type of hegemonic behaviour of the global lords raises question about their own credibility and neutrality in global affairs and creates mass-dissatisfaction in the Muslim World. Unfortunately, this approach encourages violence and creates hurdles in the promotion of global peace and prosperity.

Table: 6.1. Kashmir vs East Timor

Factor	Kashmir	East Timor
Population	13,000,000	714,000
Area (Km^2)	137,120	14,874
Dominant religion	Islam	Christianity
Occupied by a:	Non-Muslim country	Muslim country
Occupied in:	1947	1975
Number of important UN resolutions adopted	19	2
International status (solution)	Ignored by the Western bloc and the UN	Backed by the Western bloc and the UN

Source: Mirza, 2000: 110-11; East Timor, May 2000; Embassy of Pakistan (London), 2000 (unpublished); World Kashmir Freedom Movement (London), 2000 (unpublished); Embassy of Indonesia, 2000 (unpublished).

In spite of the above facts, Kashmir has consistently received little or no attention from the world community. One of the main reasons that can be cited as an explanation for this is the fact that it is a Muslim dominated territory occupied by a Non-Muslim country. This shows that religion makes a difference in how issues are perceived and ultimately dealt with. Religion is a major factor in global politics, not in the sense of spirituality but in terms of defining global alliances along ideological lines. It may be secular Turkey or the Islamic Republic of Iran or Indonesia, but the bottom line is that the population of these countries and their rulers are all predominantly Muslim and are viewed by the West through the prism of religion.

In theory, the emphasis of international politics is on the application of moral principles, however such are the levels of hypocrisy that in practice it is the interests of the major global players which determines the decisive outcome of all global decisions. This is the reason why the United Nations has given the least consideration to the Kashmir issue as compared to all other major global issues. The following table indicates the level of UN attention attributed to the Kashmir issue. It shows that the total peacekeeping force for Kashmir ranks among the lowest in the world whereas East Timor receives the highest. These figures are even more startling when we take into consideration the fact that, along with the Middle East, the Kashmir issue is the longest running problem of the post-war era.

It is noteworthy that the role of the Unites States, as in all global issues, is of vital importance. In his statement of 19th October 1999, President Clinton said: 'The United States is committed to helping the people of East Timor not only obtain the legal recognition of independence but also develop the institutions they need to thrive as an independent state' (United States Information Services, 28 September 2000). However, a month earlier, when 60 members of the US Congress, including both Republicans and Democrats, urged him to step-up actions to achieve a settlement in the Kashmir dispute by appointing a special envoy, he turned down their demand (Dawn, 11 October 1999).

This raises the question of whether this is it the right way for the United States to go about solving international problems? Is such a situation or stance beneficial in promoting global peace and prosperity? Unfortunately, it is difficult to find even a single case where the major global powers have intervened to resolve a problem in the Muslim World purely on humanitarian grounds rather than because of their own politico-economic interests.

Table: 6.2. United Nations Peacekeeping Operations

Country (issue)	Date established		Annual budget (US$ in million)
East Timor	October	1999	584.1
Sierra Leone	October	1999	504.4
Kosovo	June	1999	461.4
Bosnia	December	1995	158.7
Southern Lebanon	March	1978	146.8
Congo	December	1999	141.3
Iraq-Kuwait	April	1991	52.7
Western Sahara	September	1991	49.3
Cyprus	March	1964	43.4
Golan Heights	June	1974	37.0
Georgia	August	1993	30.0
Middle East	January	1948	23.0
India-Pakistan	January	1949	8.3
Total			2,240.4

Source: *Economist*, 5 August 2000: 26.

Palestinians – Refuge and Refusal from Water

The roots of the present dispute in the Middle East can be traced from the Zionist movement of the mid-nineteenth century, to the establishment of a Jewish homeland in Palestine, which at the time had been part of the Ottoman Empire for over four hundred years. In 1948, the Zionist leader David Ben Gurion declared Israel a Jewish state which was soon followed by a UN-mandate partitioning Palestine into two independent states one for Arabs and the other for Jews (Smith, 1996; Ovendale, 1999; Fraser, 1995). This is in spite of the fact that this region had been known as Palestine for more than two thousands years. Abdullah argued that: 'The creation of Jewish Israel in Arab Palestine was by all accounts, the most bizarre exploit of twentieth century diplomacy. It has, since 1948, blighted the lives of millions, Arabs and Jews alike, and haunted the conscience of the world community. No other international dispute has engaged the attention and energies of the United Nations throughout its history as the Palestine question and the resultant Arab-Zionist conflict. Europe's decision to solve its 'Jewish problem' at the expense of the Palestinian Arabs has evidently recoiled with destructive consequences. Many aspects of international cooperation, particularly between European and Arab countries have been adversely affected by this tragic affair. Political, economic, cultural and social relations between the countries of both regions have remained cold and frosty at the best of times' (Abdullah, 1997:5).

It is important to note that Ben Gurion himself admits the guilt of his nation by saying that: 'If I were Arab leader, I would never sign an agreement with Israel. It is normal, we have taken their country' (Dajani, 1997:8). The direct result of the establishment of this state was the displacement of tens of thousands of indigenous Palestinians. According to UN estimates, 1,200,000 Palestinians were living in the present area of Israel at the time of partition, but by the end of 1949, as many as 726,000 were forced to leave their homes (Conciliation Commission for Palestine, March 1997:7-8). The London based weekly *Economist* (27 May 2000:24) also presents similar figures and writes that between 800,000 and 900,000 Palestinians initially fled from Israel. Resolutions at the United Nation called for their right of return and the payment of compensation, but the refugees, who now number three million, were offered neither, because Israel acknowledges no responsibility for the problem. The extent of the dispersment of the Palestinian population can be judged from recent figures that show that around one million of them are living in the West Bank, 700,000 in the Gaza Strip, one and a half million in Jordan, 400,000 in Lebanon, 300,000 in Kuwait, 250,000 in Syria and nearly half a million scattered throughout other countries (Safiah, 1999: 5). One question that emerges is whether this Israeli behaviour is the outcome of the treatment which Jews themselves suffered at the hands of the medieval Muslims? A bigoted Jewish author, Carrie Supple (1993:12), admits that in medieval times 'Jews living in Muslim countries were criticised [only] for not recognising Mohammed as a prophet, but Judaism was still seen as an official religion and Jews were often protected. Indeed, many of them prospered economically and in the atmosphere of learning in the Muslim World Rabbis and scholars studied and taught the Torah, attracting students from all over the Diaspora'.

Due to the limited scope of this chapter, it is not possible to analyse the various historical facts and UN resolutions passed with regard to Palestine. The discussions in the following paragraphs serve only to highlight the suffering of Palestinians at the hands of Israel and the unwillingness of the major global players to resolve the problem on the basis of established principles. In this context, once again it would be imperative to quote a Western journal, which writes that: 'International law defines Israel as an "occupying power" in East Jerusalem and as the de facto power in West Jerusalem. ... [T]he 3.2 hectare (8 acres) of land in West Jerusalem designated for the [American] embassy...was the home of the city's richest Arabs. ... Today, Palestinian refugees and their descendants number nearly 200,000 people. Many of them live in East Jerusalem and the West Bank, some almost within sight of their former homes' (*Economist*, 5 August 2000). In another issue, the same journal (*Economist*, 22 July 2000) goes on to state that: 'Israel has ringed East Jerusalem with Jewish suburbs to ensure that the city remains united forever under Israeli sovereignty. ... But

Israel did not only annex East Jerusalem. It only extended it to about three times its original size, designing careful new boundaries that maximised the land area while minimising the number of Palestinians who lived within the city's extended borders. It then built residential colonies for Jews which, together with their linking roads, became fortresses between the West Bank and East Jerusalem. The policy of successive Israeli governments was to increase the population of Jews in East Jerusalem until they outnumbered the Arabs. They nearly succeeded.'

It is worth noting that the United States actively supports Israel's policy of occupancy. During the Camp David talks of May 2000, the then Israeli Prime Minister Ehud Barak immediately accepted President Clinton's proposal regarding the division of East Jerusalem. In reality, it was the acceptance of Israeli claims on Al-Quds. This claim was further reinforced by Israel's physical control of the city. It hardly seems to matter to Israel and the United States that this control was achieved through an act of war. Hence the overt American concerns to preserve, in theory and in practice, Israel's total sovereignty over Al-Quds. In essence, what President Clinton offered to Arafat was the sop of an office in the Muslim quarter of the walled Old City that he could call a capital without being able to claim full sovereignty over the territory. Some vaguely defined authority – but far short of sovereignty – was to be granted to Palestinians over the Muslim holy places which were to be connected to the West Bank by an overhead bridge. Some Arab villages outside the city were to be connected to the holy places and expanded to form the capital of Palestine. One cannot blame Arafat for refusing to accept this joke of an offer (*Nation*, 29 July 2000).

It needs to be emphasised that Israel's policy of expansion is not limited solely to land. This tiny country also wants to occupy and control all water resources in the region for exclusive use by

Jews. The Oxford based *New Internationalist Publications* (1999: 24-25) writes: 'This country [Israel] jealously protects its water supplies, gained in constant confrontations with Syria, Jordan and Lebanon. ... [In the West Bank, the] Arab population is totally dependent on underground water and the distribution of the resources between Palestinians and Israelis is not at all equitable. ... Palestinians on the West Banks are forced to abandon agriculture and move to cities. ... [This is why] Israeli colonists are allowed to drill wells up to 800 meters in depth, the Palestinians are not allowed to go beyond 120 meters. In 1990, according to the figures from the Israeli authorities themselves, the Palestinians of the West Bank consumed 119 cubic meter of water per head, while the Israelis consumed 354 cubic meter. The water consumption tariff system in Israel and the occupied territories also affects Palestinians and Jews differently. According to Israeli sources Palestinians pay twice the Israeli rate. The situation is more critical in the Gaza Strip where the inequality in the payment of tariffs is alarming; Palestinians pay 20 times more than the Israeli colonisers, who also receive government subsidies.'

In its analysis, the *Economist* (27 May 2000:24) also agrees with the *New Internationalist Publications'*, and states that: 'The current distribution of available water is grossly unjust. The Palestinians' use per person, in towns and for farming, is only 30% of Israelis. The settlers, profligate with irrigation, consume five or six times as much per person as their Palestinian neighbours. When it comes to drinking, 37% of West Bankers are without piped water and the Gazans drink water that is hardly fit for the fields. ... Israel's agricultural lobby is greedy and powerful; Gazans would be aghast at giving up citrus fruits or flowers. Israel controls the use of all the surface water from the Jordan and virtually all the ground water from the aquifers that criss-cross the West Bank. Its version of the future border between itself and a Palestinians state is partly dictated by its determination to keep as much control as it can.'

Does this situation reflect the justice heralded by the advocates of the contemporary process of globalisation? Did the major global players and other organisations championing human rights mount any form of protest or exert any pressure on the Jewish state to change its unjust policy? As mentioned above, Ben Gurion rightly pointed out that 'if I were Arab leader, I would never sign an agreement with Israel'.

Somalia – Destruction of a State

The experience and effects of colonialism have varied enormously throughout Africa. The Germans were efficient but brutal, violently subduing any local resistance. The Italians for their part attempted to rule by force but encountered great difficulties, as in Libya, where ten years of fighting ended with the Italians being forced to sign a peace treaty and leave the country. The French governed their colonies as part of a 'greater France', seeing them as regions and extensions of the home country. In contrast to France, Britain ruled each of its colonies separately, pursuing a divide and rule policy. In every case, the economic and social developments within African societies were severely disrupted. Agricultural and industrial production was organised for the benefit of the colonial masters; mineral wealth and raw materials were taken out of the colonies for processing, before being sold back to them as finished goods. Control was exercised from European capitals where politicians had little knowledge of African culture, and no interest in its development. A careful consideration of the current globalisation process, which in reality is a modified extension of colonisation, indicates that the same colonial aims and methodology are being used once again albeit under a different guise.

This section is based mainly on the arguments made by Chossudovsky (1998:101-09) in his book entitled, *The*

Globalisation of Poverty – Impact of IMF and the World Bank Reforms. He argued that Somalia, a country with a pastoral economy based on the 'exchange' between nomadic herdsmen and small agriculturists, was, up until the 1970s, self-sufficient in food production. Why then was its agriculture and nomadic livestock production system destroyed? In fact, nomadic pastoralists still accounted for 50 percent of the population up until 1983, with livestock contributing up to 80 percent of total export earnings.

Despite recurrent droughts, this Muslim country had continued to remain self-sufficient in the production of food up until the late 1970s. This was a situation with which the IMF and the World Bank were not entirely comfortable with. In the early 1980s, they sought to intervene in the country's domestic economy, actions which resulted in the creation of a series of crises in Somali agriculture. So-called economic reforms were imposed in a bid to transform the pastoral dominated economy into a sedentary one. Thus a very tight 'structural adjustment programme' was imposed on the government in order to release the funds required to service the country's debt. Resultantly, Somalia was forced to import food grain. From the mid-1970s to the mid-1980s, food aid increased fifteen fold at the rate of 31 percent per annum (Farzin, January 1991:265). The influx of this cheap surplus wheat and rice and its sale on the domestic market, in conjunction with the increase in commercial imports, led to the displacement of local producers, as well as to a major shift in food consumption patterns to the detriment of traditional crops, i.e., maize and sorghum. In June 1981, the IMF forced the Somali government to devalue its currency. This was followed by a series of further devaluations that pushed the price of fuel, fertilisers and farm implements up to peak levels. This led to an overall decline in the purchasing power of the general public as well as the collapse of the national economic infrastructure which had been based on agricultural and livestock production.

Chossudovsky (1998) argues that the 'hidden objective' of this programme was to eliminate the nomadic herdsmen involved in the traditional exchange economy. The collapse in veterinarian services also indirectly served the interests of the major global players as evidenced by the fact that in 1984 Somalian cattle exports to Saudi Arabia and the Gulf countries were replaced by beef imports from Australia and the EU countries. In these circumstances, the donors provided increased 'aid', not in the form of imports of capital and equipment, but in the form of 'food aid'. The extreme dependency on food aid enabled the donors to take control of the entire budgetary process. The IMF-World Bank backed economic reforms resulted in the disintegration of health and educational programmes. By 1989, expenditure on health had declined by 78 percent from its 1975 level.

This situation indicates that it was the IMF-World Bank programme which led the Somali economy into a vicious circle – the decimation of the herds pushed the nomadic pastoralists close to starvation which in turn impacted on grain producers who sold or bartered their grain for cattle. The entire social fabric of the pastoralist economy was undone. The collapse in foreign exchange earnings from declining cattle exports, and Somali workers remittances from Gulf countries, adversely affected the balance of payments and the states public finances leading to the breakdown of the government's economic and social programmes. Chossudovsky further argues that although 'external' climatic variables play a role in triggering off a famine and heightening the social impact of drought; famines in the age of globalisation are mostly man-made. They are not the consequence of 'a scarcity of food' but of a structure of global oversupply which undermines food security and destroys national agricultural systems.

One of the main reasons behind the desire to punish Somalia was that its autocratic President, General Siad Barre, had adopted Marxist policies that were not popular with Western countries. Furthermore, the United States, along with the other global powers, were particularly interested in Somalia due to its strategic position on the Horn of Africa. This country is situated at the point where the Red Sea meets the Indian Ocean, close to the oilfields of the Persian Gulf and those of Saudi Arabia. The access to oil resources was an important factor in determining the Western powers decision to intervene in Somalian affairs. Once again, it is the politico-economic interests of the makers and breakers of global maps that form the main issues of concern in the global arena. This seems to be a fact lost on many in the global media who tend to present a distorted picture of events. The global images and reports that the Western media chose to show merely served to highlight the human suffering caused by the civil war and droughts rather than seeking to expose the real causes of this tragedy. Such reporting keeps the Western public in a state of ignorance as to the real causes of events and ultimately succeeds in preserving the status quo. The above discussion also shows that there are many other 'Somalias' in the Muslim World and unless the ruling elites in Muslim countries read the writing on the wall, their future too, will become one of uncertainty.

Sanctions on Iraq – A Weapon of Mass Destruction

A decade after the Iraqi invasion of Kuwait, a situation now exists in Iraq where the American led UN sanctions have taken a terrible toll on the innocent civilian population. The purpose and effectiveness of these sanctions must be questioned given the fact that Saddam Hussein, 'the source of all evils' in the eyes of Washington, has continued to remain in power. Indeed, his hold on power has been strengthened rather than weakened by this unrelenting outside pressure. Despite the fact that a majority of Iraqis are opposed to the *Ba'athist* dictator, their opposition to the United States and the United Kingdom, whose fighter jets continue to fly overhead and engage in bombing raids, is much stronger. It would not be wrong to say that the Mongols attack on Baghdad in the medieval age and Baghdad's attack on Kuwait in the modern age constituted the most significant incidents in the destruction of a belief in a Muslim *Ummah*. It still remains unclear as how this loss will be ever be recovered, or how the people in Kuwait will forget the brutalities carried out against them by the Iraqi Army (Sasson, 1991; Mckinnon and Vine, 1991; Parliamentary Human Rights Group, 1991; Centre for Research and Studies on Kuwait, 1996).

However, the fact remains that there can be no justification for the continued punishment of 22 million innocent civilians for the crimes of a dictatorial ruler. This was the reason that Jutta Purghart, the third United Nations official-in-charge of the 'oil for food programme' in Iraq, cited when resigning from her position in February 2000. The previous occupants of the post, Denis Halliday and Hans von Sponeck, had also resigned from the same sense of futility and outrage. It is stark commentary on the effects of the US-maintained sanctions that even the international humanitarian officials cannot tolerate the agony that these sanctions have wrought on Iraq's infrastructure and civilian population (Said, 4 March 2000). The *Economist* (8 April 2000:22, 26) writes: 'Slowly, inexorably, a generation is being crushed in Iraq. Thousands are dying, thousands more are leading stunted lives, and storing up bitter hatreds for the future. … Hospitals display the effects of the embargo at their most tragic. Iraq's health services, like its schools, were once the best in the region. Now most hospital lifts have ceased to functions, so trauma patients have to be carried up and down the stairs. Medicine, too, is rationed. Whole wards of children with leukaemia go unattended, since the different drugs needed to treat them are rarely available. Diseases such as cholera and typhoid, which had been eradicated before 1990, have reappeared. The Iraqi authorities, doubtless with an eye to the headlines, recently claimed that more than a million people had died as a result of the embargo. But the more cautious studies of foreign researchers show horrific rises in infant mortality, malnutrition and disease. An analysis of NGO health surveys conducted by Richard Garfield, a public health expert at Columbia University, found that at least 100,000 (and probably as many as 227,000) children under-five had died between 1991 and 1998 as a result of sanctions. That works out at between 26 and 60 deaths every day among infants alone. A recent Unicef report estimated that, over the same period, some 500,000 children under-five had died.'

Another issue of the *Economist* (8 April 2000: 22) blames Saddam Hussein, not the Western countries or the United Nations, for all the sufferings of his people. However, this magazine of international repute does not provide any justification, or cite any international law or a moral principle, that allows a whole nation to be punished for the misdeeds of one man. Why are the global champions of human rights silent on the deaths of 500,000 infants? Is it because these children are somehow linked to 'Saddam's military machine' or because they were going to grow up to be the 'Muslim fundamentalists' of the future? In order to gain a sense of perspective it is perhaps appropriate to quote a comparative example as a means of assessing the extent to which the Western media are concerned with the continued deaths of tens of thousands of Iraqi infants. During the first half of 2000, a six years old boy, Elian Gonzales, became one of the hottest news stories issues in the American press and electronic media (*New York Times*, 6, 23 January, 14 February 2000; *Economist*, 15 and 22 January, 22 and 29 April, 13, 27 May, 1 and 29 July 2000). Elian's mother, along with a number of other asylum seekers fleeing Cuba, drowned when the boat in which she was travelling capsized off the coast of America. However, Elian survived the ordeal and his American relatives were desperate to keep him in America rather than send him back to Cuba to live with his father. For several months the situation remained tense with various human rights organisations and political lobbies strongly protesting any attempts to return the child to Cuba. The seriousness of the situation forced Vie-President Al-Gore (who at that time was beginning his campaign to become the next president of the United States) to pander to Cuban-American votes by calling for Elian and his father to stay in the United States (*Economist*, 22 April, 23 August 2000). This situation raises the question as to whether the 'residence' of a Cuban child is an issue of greater importance than the lives of millions of Iraqi children? Can the Iraqi children expect the American media to raise their voices in support of their rights to life?

A renowned journalist John Pilger (2000:60) revealed that 'in May 1996, the US Secretary of State Madeleine Albright was asked on the CBS programme *60 Minutes* if the deaths of more than half a million children was a price worth paying for the continued imposition of sanctions. "[W]e think the price is worth it", she replied'. The previously mentioned former United Nations Assistant Secretary General and Humanitarian Coordinator Denis J. Halliday (1999:55-56), argued that apart from other losses 'the social cost of sanctions has been enormous. Iraqi females and Islamic family values have been damaged. Children have been forced to work, to become street kids, to beg and engage in crime. Young women have been forced into prostitution by the desperation of their families. Fathers have abandoned their families. The many problems single mothers already faced in the aftermath of the Iran-Iraq war have been compounded. Workplace progress that professionals and other women had achieved in recent decades has been lost. The education system has collapsed with thousands of teachers leaving their posts because they are unable to work under existing conditions and a dropout rate of some 30 percent exits at primary and secondary levels. The health services are unable to handle the most basic and preventable diseases such as diarrhoea, gastroenteritis, respiratory tract infections and polio. Hospitals attempt to function with collapsed water and sewage systems, without even the basic supplies needed for hygiene and the minimal level of care. ... Studies show that sanctions almost always fail to achieve their stated objectives. They tend to miss a country's leadership and hit the innocent. They impact most on democratic societies, but fail to impress the dictatorial regimes whose leaders often remain untouched with civilians paying the price.'

Sudan – Another Victim of American Fundamentalism

The above discussion indicates that the major global players, and particularly the United States, apply United Nations resolutions if and when they are deemed necessary to protect their global interests. They are particularly hostile with regard to the Muslim World. The UN has no designated role in Palestine as UN resolutions state that Palestinians have the right to return to their homeland. Furthermore, these resolutions also state that Israel should vacate the occupied territories, a move it has so far refused to undertake. The same is also true of Kashmir where the United Nations feels paralysed. However, in East Timor, the situation has been shown to be the opposite. Here the quick and strict implementation of UN resolutions served the interests of Christians in creating a new homeland whilst at the same time destabilising the largest Muslim country in the Islamic World. The situation of Iraq could also be said to exhibit similar characteristics.

This final section provides one further example of American interference in the affairs of a Muslim country; the attack on a medicine factory in Sudan. The UN was paralysed to investigate whether this could be deemed a terrorist attack or a genuine effort to crackdown on a factory which was making nerve-gas for use in mass killings (Gabb, 1998; The National Scientific Committee – Sudan, unpublished). The civil war in Sudan has received a lot of propagandist coverage in the Western media, with several reports being published by various international organisations, including Amnesty International (*Amnesty-Human Rights Worldwide*, 2000:12)[2], detailing serious human rights abuses. However, neither the champions of human rights nor the Western media advocated a United Nations investigation or the establishment of an impartial international tribunal in response to US actions in the country. The reason for this silence can be attributed to the highly influential role and position of dominance occupied by the United States in global affairs.

On the 20th August 1998, US forces launched a missile attack on the Al-Shifa pharmaceutical factory in Northern Khartoum, which killed and wounded civilians and caused the total destruction to the factory and its equipment. It is beyond doubt that this air strike against a civil industrial target in Sudan was a grave and flagrant transgression of international law. The destruction of this pharmaceutical plant also caused a severe shortage of lifesaving medicines needed to prevent the deaths, from easily treatable diseases, of thousands of adults and children in hospitals around the country. Sudan called for an urgent investigation by the Security Council into this unprovoked act of aggression and invited the UN to send a technical team to examine the factory in order to verify the American claims. The US Administration obstructed the undertaking of such measures and refused to consent to proposals urging for the matter to be taken to the International Court of Justice (Sudan Foundation, October 2000).

Furthermore, instead of providing concrete proof that the factory was indeed involved in making lethal nerve-gas, and calling for the dispute to be settled through the appropriate international channels, the American press continued to defend its government's action. For instance, the *New York Times* wrote that: 'In the 14 months since President Clinton ordered a cruise missile attack on a pharmaceutical plant in Sudan, his aides have steadfastly defended the decision' (Risen, 27 October 1999).

This claim is denied by the weekly *Economist* (26 August 2000:58) which states that 'no evidence has been produced [by the American government] that the plant was making lethal chemicals'. However, in spite of this fact, the US Under Secretary of State Thomas Pickering (Gabb, 1998) dismissed the need for an independent investigation of the site. He went on to insist that the American position is clear and persuasive. This refusal to countenance an international investigation occurred in spite of the fact that a British engineer Tom Carnaffin (Gabb, 1998), who was engaged in the construction and equipping of the factory, stated that: 'I have intimate knowledge of that factory and it just does not lend itself to the manufacture of chemical weapons. ... I have intimate knowledge of every part of the establishment and unless there have been some radical changes in the past few months it isn't equipped to cope with the demands of chemical weapons manufacturing. You need things like airlocks but that factory just has doors leading out onto the street.'

In fact, rather than permitting a fair and impartial investigation to take place, the United States accelerated its propaganda war and argued that Sudan, Iraq and Osama Bin Laden, all had close links in the production of chemical weapons (*New York Times*, 24 and 26 August, 4, 24 and 26 October, 6 and 26 September 1998). In addition, the United States was also seen to be supporting Sudan's rebels in the ensuing civil war. In 1999, Jane Perlez wrote in the *New York Times* (29 November 1999) that: 'President Clinton is about to sign a bill permitting the administration to pursue a contentious strategy against the Islamic government in Sudan by giving assistance directly to rebels who have been fighting the authorities in Khartoum'. Is this the way American justice is pursued in the contemporary globalised world?

Notes:

[1] For example, the resolution adopted by the UN Commission for India and Pakistan in 1949 and Security Council's resolutions No. 38, 39, 47 and 51 (1948), 80 (1950), 91 and 96 (1951), 98 (1952), 122, 123 and 126 (1957), 209, 210, 211, 214 and 215 (1965), 303 and 307 (1971).

[2] During the period 1996-2000, out of a total of 14 website news reports from Amnesty International, only one was related to the US air strikes on Sudan. Even in this one report, Amnesty refused to criticise the US attacks instead it politely expressed its concern over the issue. It states that: 'Amnesty International expressed its alarm at yesterday's United States air strikes on targets in Afghanistan and Sudan.' The rest of the one page news report was mainly concerned with a condemnation of Sudan and Afghanistan. Furthermore, in its issue of September-October, the *Amnesty – Human Rights Worldwide* (an Amnesty's journal), condemns nearly three dozen countries for their poor record on human rights. The majority of these countries belong to the Muslim World. Today Muslim countries account for less than one third of the world's countries and only around a quarter of the total global population. Why then is the Muslim World consistently considered to be more violent than the Non-Muslim World? Are there specific lobbies with set agendas working to create a bad image of Islam?

7

Another Cold War - Information, Technology and Global Media

In the modern world, the advancements in the field of information technology have become an important instrument for Western industrial countries in their desire to control global affairs. However, of perhaps more significance is the marriage between information technology and the global media system, which plays a critical role in forming and shaping international public opinion. In fact, this information technology and global media system is almost exclusively owned by a set of Western corporations, e.g., Agence France Press, Associated Press, Reuters, News Corporation and Viacom etc., who in turn all hold vested interests in the World Bank, IMF and the WTO. Indeed, none of corporations in the business of information and news diffusion come from Asia, Africa, South or Central America, or any of the developing countries. The World Bank (1999), indicates that the 'technological advances in communication have made it possible to know in an instant what is happening in a household or factory, or on a stock market half a world away. The growing importance of information services in the world economy means that an increasing proportion of economic value is weightless. This means that information can now be transmitted faster, cheaper and with much greater ease through the use of fibre-optic cables. At the same time improvements in transportation networks and technology are reducing the costs of shipping goods by sea, ground, and air, and improvements in information technology have made it easier to manage these new interconnections.' However, are these aforementioned benefits being shared equally amongst all the countries of the world? According to the UNDP (1999), the current developments in the field of information and technology are in fact widening the gap between the world's 'haves' and 'have-nots'. The report reveals that in major OECD countries, more than half of their GDP is knowledge based. This new technology has replaced manual labour, which in turn has adversely affected the position of the developing world due to the fact that it does not possess the necessary skills and knowledge needed to compete. It is this skill that forms the core element in achieving success in the new global market. The report (UNDP, 1999: 1, 5, 6, 57) states that:

- Globalisation is not new, but the present era shows distinctive features. Shrinking space, shrinking time and disappearing borders are linking people's lives more deeply, more intensively, and more immediately than ever before.

- New information and communications technologies are driving the globalisation process, but polarising the world into the connected and the isolated.

- Poor people and poor countries risk being pushed to the margins by this proprietary regime that controls the world's knowledge.

- Global technological breakthroughs offer a great potential for human advancement and the eradication of poverty – but not with today's agendas.

- The global gap between haves and have-nots, between know and know-nots, is widening.

What are the reasons and explanation for this widening gap? According to Schenker (1999:56): 'The consequences of this technology lag are serious, because over the next decade, 30% of the world's economic growth and 40% of new employment will be driven by information technology. A plethora of new initiatives has emerged to try to close the gap, but opinions differ about what donor organisations should do to help roll out telecommunications to the developing world. ... For some schools the internet means expanding horizons, but others worry it will divert resources away from hiring teachers. Analysts agree that it is unrealistic to expect that every family can be equipped with a computer – or even that every home can be linked to the telecommunications infrastructure or an electricity grid. The UN report notes that buying a personal computer costs the average US citizen about a month's pay, compared to eight years' worth of wages for a citizen of Bangladesh.' Under such circumstances it becomes impossible to see how the Muslim countries can even begin to start reducing this widening communications technology gap. This leads to a situation where they become unable to compete in the global market and where their domestic markets become even more accessible and vulnerable to further exploitation from western corporations.

Information Technology – Where does the Muslim World Stand?

The following table reflects the overall picture of the level of internet use throughout the different regions of the world. The figures show that the highest level of internet use was in the United States (26%) followed by the OECD countries (7%). In the regions of the South and South East Asia, the Middle East and North Africa, where most Muslim countries are situated, the use of internet was minimal. In South Asia, where two of the most highly populated Muslim countries, i.e., Bangladesh and Pakistan, are situated, internet use was recorded at only 0.04 percent as against the world average of 2.4 percent. This indicates that the use of internet in this region was 60 times less than the world average. Similarly, in the oil rich Arab states, internet use was calculated to be twelve times less than the world average. When compared with the United States, the difference is made all the more stark as the figures for South Asia and the Arab states stand at 1:658 and 1:132, respectively. In light of this trend how many decades would be required for these regions to reach the existing level of the United States? Indeed, if this level were ever achieved it would perhaps prove incidental as the gap by that time would have widened even further due to the continuing speed of technological advancements in the United States.

It is noteworthy that there are various other factors linked with the progress and extensive use of internet in a country or region. Particularly, the level of literacy, income, cultural values and the nature and level of consumption of a society are the most important factors in this regard. The analysis made in the previous chapters reflect that in the process of development, the Muslim World is far behind as compared to the Non-Muslim World, therefore, it will take them a long time to achieve the existing level of the Non-Muslim World. The same is also true in the case of the use of internet where the sustained efforts are required to acquire the maximum benefit of this important source of information and technology. Otherwise, the digital divide will keep on expanding and the Muslim World will be marginalised in process of globalisation. The leadership of the Muslim World has to understand this fact and efforts should be made in this regard.

Table: 7.1. Internet Users – A Global Enclave

Regions/country/ Organisation	Regional population (as a % of world population)	Internet Users (as a % of regional population)
United States	4.7	26.3
OECD (excluding U.S.)	14.1	6.9
Latin America and The Caribbean	6.8	0.8
South East Asia and the Pacific	8.6	0.5
East Asia	22.2	0.4
Eastern Europe and the CIS	5.8	0.4
Arab States	4.5	0.2
Sub-Saharan Africa	9.7	0.1
South Asia	23.5	0.04
World	100	2.4

Source: UNDP, 1999: 63.

Note: The Czech Republic, Hungary, Mexico, Poland, the Republic of Korea and Turkey are included in the OECD and not in the regional aggregates.

It needs to be re-emphasised here that, as in all the other fields of daily life, the Muslim World also lags far behind the Non-Muslim in the use of modern information technology. The following table indicates that in the case of high-income countries, the Muslim World has nearly half of the television sets per 1000 people as compared to the Non-Muslim World. This ratio further declines with regard to the use of computers and the internet, where the ratios for the Muslim and the Non-Muslim worlds were around 1:5 and 1:29, respectively. In the case of low-income countries the picture becomes bleaker for the Muslim World as the ratios for the use of television, computer and the internet between the Muslim and the Non-Muslim Worlds were 1:2.5, 1:5.4 and 1:46, respectively. Under such circumstances, how can the Muslim World be expected to make progress when it is so far behind the rest of the world in the use of modern communication technology? It also reflects the fact that the above mentioned UNDP statements from its 1999 report, present a true assessment of developments in the Muslim World.

Table: 7.2. The Use of Television, Computer and Internet
in the Muslim and the Non-Muslim Worlds

(per 1000 people)

Countries	No. of television sets	No. of computers	No. of internet users
Muslim World			
• High-income countries	318.72	42.50	2.14
• Low-income countries	89.93	7.91	0.08
Non-Muslim World			
• High-income countries	623.41	221.32	62.70
• Low-income countries	225.20	36.41	3.60

Source: Computed from UNDP, 1999: 53-56, 166-67, 193.

Propaganda and Publicity

It is important to note that, despite its huge potential and the fact that it is a formidable force in world affairs, the Muslim World still continues to suffer from a whole host of problems throughout most parts of the globe; from North and East Africa to the Middle East, Central and East Asia, and even in Europe. Islam is being branded as a reactionary force and is portrayed as the enemy of Western civilisation. The Western media has raised the threatening spectre of 'Islamic fundamentalism' and 'Muslim terrorism' and is wary of resurgent movements in the Muslim World. Koreshi (1995) argues that: 'The two most prominent examples of recent days are the coined words 'fundamentalism' and 'terrorism', which have become the new words of abuse for Islam and Muslim liberation movements. One can look at the terms that have been used over the years for Islamic resurgence. It started with 'militant Islam' then it became 'radical Islam' then 'fundamentalism' and then 'Islamism' and 'Islamic zealots'. So pervasive have been their use that out of naivety the Muslims are using these abusive words for themselves. The West does not describe the Islamic trend as Islamic nationalism, or Muslim brotherhood, for this description would have some favourable connotations. ... The American attempts to equate Islamism with terrorism are at best devious. So successful have they been in this distortion exercise that almost every one has taken the new currency of terrorism for liberation struggle. ... Demolishing unacceptable leaders, regimes and lionising the favourites through the media is a proven Western method.'

Throughout the course of this hostile propaganda campaign, and through the use of such self-created issues as women rights, human rights and terrorism, the Western World seems to have forgotten its own recent past. In this context, Ali Mazrui (1997: 120-27) argues that British women 'were only granted the right to own property independent of their husbands in 1870, while Muslim women have always had that right. Indeed, Islam is the only religion in the world to be preached by and emanate from a businessman in commercial partnership with his wife. Islamic law has always allocated that shares from every inheritance be passed to both daughters and sons.' He further reveals that:

- In almost all Western countries, except for New Zealand, women did not gain the right to vote until the twentieth century. Great Britain extended the vote to women in two stages in 1918, and 1928, and the United States enfranchised them by constitutional amendments in 1920. France followed as recently as 1944. Switzerland did not permit women to vote in national elections until 1971 – decades after Muslim women in Afghanistan, Iran and Pakistan had been casting ballots.

- No woman has ever risen to become the president of USA. In contrast three Muslim countries, Pakistan, Bangladesh and Turkey have all had women prime ministers [and the president in Indonesia, the most populous Muslim country, is also a woman].

- Muslim societies have not conducted organised massacres and engaged in fascism. There are no Muslim equivalents to Nazi concentration camps, nor Muslim conquests through genocide on the scale perpetrated by Europeans in America and Australia. Nor is there a Muslim equivalent to Stalinist terror, or Pol Pot's killing fields. Nor are there Muslim versions of apartheid like that once approved by the South African Dutch Reformed Church, or the ferocious racism of Japan before 1945, or the racist culture of the old South in the United States, with its lynching and brutalization of black people. Furthermore, Islam has not been responsible for dropping two nuclear bombs of mass destruction.

The problem between Islam and the West is not so much one of values but one of perceptions and prejudices that blur views and perspectives. It is this factor that has lead to the projection of Islamic fundamentalism as a perceived threat that acts as a convenient manipulative mechanism in a bid to maximise geopolitical and geo-economic dividends. 'During the Cold War, the Western powers used Islam as a means of undermining Communism in Central Asia. During the 1920s, the British in India supported the Basmachis by providing them with guns and money. In 1930, British agents infiltrated Afghanistan and India in order to whip up Islamic feelings in Central Asia. Fitzroy Maclean, a British diplomat and secret agent, advised his government, in a secret memorandum in October 1939, that they should attempt to destabilise Central Asia by using its *Mullahs* to prevent Russia from invading Turkey and Iran. In 1979, the USA used the Afghan war to spread Islam in Central Asia for the purpose of undermining Communism' (Rashid, 1994:245).

However, the tables were turned following the withdrawal of Soviet troops from Afghan soil. 'The same *Mujahideen* who had previously been portrayed as freedom fighters were now dubbed fundamentalists to be despised and condemned. When the US Secretary of State James Baker visited Central Asia, he gave a firm warning to the governments of Central Asia to stay away from the radical Islamists and not let the influence of Afghanistan and Iran creep into Central Asia. Fundamentalism is thus a functional tool – a double-edged sword to be used either way as expediency dictates. In the context of Central Asia, the projected evils of fundamentalism are being blown out of all proportion' (Beg, 1998). 'Initial apprehension, both in Moscow and Washington, about the threat of Islamic fundamentalism from these Republics has proven to be exaggerated and ill-founded. The region has not witnessed the kind of competitive conflict forecast by many Western observers, who envisaged fighting between Iran and Turkey, or Iran and Saudi Arabia, or Pakistan and Iran, in order to regain the Islamic world's lost heritage which had been rediscovered with the collapse of Communism in the Soviet Union' (Hussain, 11 February 1996).

'Islamisation' of International Aid?

A number of examples of the propaganda used against Muslim countries can be quoted here as points of reference. For instance, Gust (1999) has criticised any international aid that is linked with Islam. He argued that the aid given to these recipient countries, often causes little or no fundamental change because it is given for the satisfaction of spiritual desires rather than economic development. He specifically criticised Saudi Arabia because it sent free Qurans to some of Muslim countries. Likewise, after the collapse of the Soviet Union, the governments of the Islamic Republic of Iran and Saudi Arabia sent copies of the Quran as a gift to the people of the six newly established republics in Central Asia. Such criticism raises some important points with regard to the issue of 'Islamic aid':

- While it is a matter of common knowledge that various organisations of different religions provide religious material to developing countries, why was it only the distribution of the Quran that was criticised?

- Was Gust ignorant of the fact that all religions of the world preach love, peace and prosperity, and that they fulfil the spiritual needs of their followers, which in many instances are no less important than their materialistic needs?

- The reality is that in every sphere of life the situation of Muslim countries cannot be compared with Non-Muslim countries, as in the former it is believed that Islam is a complete code of life while in the latter religion is considered a personal matter.

- It is a historical fact that countries, communities and individuals prefer to interact with each other where they feel there is some common ground for interaction. The same is also true for a Muslim country that provides aid to satisfy the basic spiritual needs of the people of a recipient country. Is such a situation harmful to global peace and prosperity?

- Although, such aid may not meet the standards laid-down by Western donors, the Muslim recipient communities often consider such help to be vitally important.

- From the Western point of view, this aid may not have an immediate economic impact, however, in reality it has more potential for socio-economic development and the promotion of religio-cultural relations between the donor and recipient countries because it is based on a shared history, religion and culture. This situation is in turn supportive to the promotion of human development, global peace and prosperity.

Redrafting the Global Map

Today the map of the Muslim World has little ethnic, religious or socio-linguistic validity in the world as it arose merely as a result of colonial division. It seems that the major global players are still fearful of the fragments that emerged from the destruction of the vast Ottoman and Persian Empires. This can be cited as one of the reasons as to why they are still attempting to further disintegrate these pieces. In 1995, Koreshi highlighted this point by referring to the fact that Pakistan, generally see as one of the most important of the Islamic countries, and was being singled out for particularly harsh attention and scrutiny. This situation indicates that the activities of the major powers and the United States in particular are not just limited to propagating anti-Muslim propaganda but are in fact dedicated to the reshaping and restructuring of the entire Muslim World. In chapter five, reference was made to a report in which the US predicted that Pakistan would disintegrate over the coming two decades, and that Iran and India would go to war as a result in a bid to gain territorial advantage. The report highlighted that Pakistan may collapse due to an economic crisis and India will move to annex all the territory of the state of Jammu and Kashmir. It is believed that this action will subsequently lead to the complete disintegration and disappearance of Pakistan, and the creation of an expanded Indian Confederation or a super state. The Report further states that the United States will intervene to destroy Pakistan's nuclear installations. The launching of air strikes (to destroy Pakistani nuclear facilities) will save the nuclear weapons from falling into the hands of zealots (*Dawn*, 17 September 2000).

Is the reshaping of regional maps part and parcel of the current globalisation process? Chossudovsky (1998: 101-09, 243-63) also agrees with Koreshi (1995) and follows his line of thinking in producing facts that seek to explain the destruction of Somalia, the disintegration of the former Yugoslavia and the suffering of the people of Bosnia-Herzegovina. He exposed the hidden realities and highlighted the reasons behind the civil wars. His findings showed that when the major global powers want to make or break a country, they first of all set about creating a particular environment with which to work in. There are many examples of this created environment, from the Camp-David accord between Egypt and Israel to the war between Iran and Iraq, from the Gulf War to the imposed sanctions on Iraq, and from Bosnia-Herzegovina to the emergence of East Timor.

Ignoring the Real Problems and Exaggerating Political Issues

It is common knowledge that the Western media is ignoring the real problems of Muslim countries and deprived Muslim communities across the world, and choosing instead to focus on political issues of a secondary or tertiary importance. The case of Myanmar's Ruhangya refugees can be presented a good example in this regard. According to Abdus Samad (1994: 195-96): 'This case is completely different from any other known refugee case, both in nature and manner, because it is a question of identity and of the indigenousness of a race called the Ruhangya, who inhabit the Arakan province. These extremely under-privileged and ill-fated people have no written history of their own, and Burmese historians have completely neglected them assuming them immigrants, and not an indigenous people. This assumption, according to Inamullah Khan, the Secretary General of the World Muslim Congress, is 'a lie which has to be nailed' ... Unlike the Palestinian and Afghan refugee problems, this case is almost unknown to the global community.'

The objective of the above discussion is not to prove the indigenous rights of the Ruhangya Muslim people, who have been living on this land for centuries, but to highlight the fact that because this problem is related to a Muslim community, it is thus ignored by the global media. The suffering and misery of these people has been overshadowed by other politico-democratic issues raised by the international community in relation to events in Burma. Abdus Samad (1994) reveals that, in 1978, the Burmese government started an operation in which these people were taken in-groups to local police stations on the pretext of checking their national identity cards, which then were torn to pieces in a bid to deny them a documented legal identity. During this operation the Burmese soldiers set-up light machine-gun posts and on a number of occasions fired upon Muslim refugees on the Bangladesh border. These refugees were later repatriated under an agreement reached between the Bangladeshi and Burmese governments. However, the same atrocity was repeated again in 1991, and as a result nearly 300,000 Ruhangyas are now living in disease-ridden camps in Bangladesh - a life of eviction, deprivation and raggedness.

The international media which has consistently focused on the Buddhist opposition leader Aung San Suu Kyi, never cared to draw global attention to the above mentioned merciless attacks and continued human rights violations committed by the Military regime of this country against its own innocent and defenceless people. Sadly, the Amnesty International report on Burma, produced in November 1994, contained no reference to the issue. The same is also true for various other reports which focus on the human rights situation of this country with respect to democracy rather the miseries of tens of thousands of its people. There was one report on the internet (entitled: *Report(s) on Human Rights Situation in Burma – 1*, [http:// www. falcon. cc. ukans. edu/~jrchien /politics /report-on -human. html] July 2000) which discussed all issues of human rights violations and democracy in Burma as well as Thailand, but remained silent on the issue of Arakan. Another detailed report issued by the US Department of State (February 2000), briefly touched on the issue by mentioning a few words on the problem.

Islam or 'Islamophobia'?

The misunderstandings concerning Islam and the Muslim World, and the barrage of global media propaganda, have created an environment of mutual distrust between the Muslim and the Non-Muslim worlds (particularly the Western World). The Western press, especially various American and British newspapers, play a leading role in presenting a negative image of Islam. In 1992, a 'London *Times* cartoon showed a Muslim wiping a blood-stained sword on a union flag, with a murdered woman behind him' (Fisk, 2000: 13-14). Is this the picture of Islam which the West wants to project? As mentioned above, the Muslim World is particularly irritated by the global media's use of certain terms of categorisation such as, fundamentalism, terrorism, isolation, and rouge state. In many cases the governments of most Muslim countries spend an inordinate amount of their time and energy trying to prove that they are not supporting fundamentalism and terrorism.

The imposition of international 'isolation' status and 'sanctions' on certain countries has proved to be not only harmful to the Muslim World but also to humankind in general. The economic deprivation and sufferings imposed upon a country through the policies of containment, isolation and sanctions result in frustration and disparity. Iran, Iraq, Sudan and Afghanistan are only a few examples in this regard. Abdul Qader Tash (22 June 1997), editor in chief of the Arab News, in referring to the Western media image of Islam, states that: 'A distorted image of Islam and Arabs has unfortunately been a feature of the American media for over a century. According to Professor Jack Shaheen of the University of Southern Illinois (author of *The TV Arab* and internationally recognised authority on the subject of anti-Arab and anti-Islam stereotypes in the US), in the past 100 years, Hollywood has produced more than 700 films whose contents vilify Islam and Arabs. Extending his study beyond Hollywood films, Shaheen also examined more than 250 comic books published during the past 50 years. He also looked at hundreds of children's cartoons and more than 450 children's films, from an early one in 1893 to Walt Disney's *Aladdin* in 1993. [In his own words], [h]is conclusion is: 'My research has indicated that the term 'Arab' and 'Muslim' draw a hostile reaction from the public as they find it difficult to differentiate between reality and imagination. Perhaps no people anywhere in the world, other than 270 million Arabs, have been so grossly misunderstood. Similarly Islam, the faith of over a billion Muslims, including 6-8 million in the United States, is the religion that has suffered more than any other because of general ignorance about it.'

Tash (22 June 1997) further argued that: 'The religion [Islam] and its followers are being maligned. The systematic distortion of their image is no longer a minor irritant that can be ignored.

Some of those who have made a study of this phenomenon call it 'Islamophobia', indicating thereby that the campaign has its roots in a morbid fear of Islam and that in the course of time, it will arouse the same fear in the public mind. The end result they believe will be the creation of a climate of hatred and distaste in these societies for everything Islamic. A number of Western thinkers and intellectuals have begun addressing the problem and warning people of its consequences. One such warning came recently from Professor Gordon Conway of Sussex University in Britain. Discussing the issue, he said that a careful look at the print media in particular would show the extent of anti-Muslim sentiments. In tabloids, he pointed out, the attack against Islam was usually harsh and savage while in more respected papers it was subtler.'

Anti-Islamic sentiments have increasingly become more publicly pronounced following the global resurgence of Islam. The above discussion reflects the real picture of the global situation in which a negative picture of Muslims and Islam is being painted. This is one of the main reasons for the Muslim population all over the world continuing to suffer, more so than any other religion, from injustice. This situation can also be seen in *Economist – Millennium Special Edition* (31 December 1999: 135), in which a picture of God was published along with the following comments: 'After a lengthy career, the Almighty recently passed into history. ... Few ordinary folk, though they had different names for him, doubted the reality of God. He was up there somewhere (up, not down; in his long career, no one ever located him on the seabed), always had been, always should be. ... Yet why bother with proof, if everyone knew it anyway? One, because great brains are like that; two, because not everyone did. Out there were the gentiles, Saracens and such. But did not they too say, "There is no God but God".' In fact, anybody having even the slightest knowledge of Islam can clearly understand the meaning of this statement, the last sentence in particular. Is this not a direct attack on Islam or merely a polite way of insulting the second largest religion in the world?

This is not just the result of systematic propaganda. Ahsan (1988:109) argues that under current global circumstances, Muslim views and news are either neglected or misinterpreted by the Western media. This is exacerbated by the fact that, due to their own weak media and information technology, Muslim countries are totally dependent upon the Western World, not only to communicate with 'them' but also to be able to communicate among themselves. How has the Muslim World found itself in such a situation and what can it do to rectify the situation? One of the most important factors is that the global media power unleashed against the Muslim World is causing unprecedented danger to the unity and self-respect of this world. As is evident from the above discussion, this media, which is completely owned by the West and acting in its interests, has adopted the strategy of over-exaggeration in its dealings with the Muslim World. One of its main objectives is to malign Islam and Islamists by pursuing a strategy of categorising the Muslim World, through the repetition of a series of stock phrases that have become embedded in peoples consciousness as defining terms, when dealing with issues related to Islam and Muslims. The treatment being meted out to Sudan, Afghanistan, Iran, Libya, Algeria, Iraq, Pakistan and Indonesia are examples of anti-Islamic policy. To overcome this malaise, the Muslim World needs to take stock of this deteriorating situation and evolve measures for setting its own house in order. This situation demands a common strategy for the development and formation of a powerful media system specifically designed by and for the Muslim World. This will not only help to project the Muslim cause in the world but will also counter the misinformation being unleashed by a hostile Western media.

At present there are two Islamic news agencies (i.e., IINA and ISBO), both established by the OIC. The IINA was established in 1970, and its main objectives were; to promote close relations and technical cooperation among the news agencies of member states, and to create an environment of better understanding among Muslim peoples of their common politio-economic and social problems. Due to a series of financial crises, the IINA failed to establish its own communications network and has had to sign a contract with a Rome-based company to broadcast its news through a high frequency radio transmitter. Unfortunately, these news broadcasts are not directly accessible to either the public or the news agencies of the member states. The ISBO was established in 1975, with similar objectives to the IINA. This agency does not broadcast directly but produces a limited number of, primarily radio, programmes for its member states (Ahsan, 1988: 38-40). In fact the spectrum of activities of both of these agencies is very limited and they have had no impact in presenting the Muslim cause to the global world.

In fact, the news media is a crucial issue in Muslim countries, as instead of sharing news and information amongst themselves, they buy news from major news cartels such as Reuter, Agence France Press and Associated Press. In Muslim countries, there is a lack of mutual cooperation in the sharing, distribution and diffusion of news, a problem that does not exist in western-based new agencies. Here, close cooperation between the Muslim media and the Western based new agencies is required. Unfortunately, this cooperation does not exist and instead of promoting mutual contacts between the media and news agencies of the Muslim and the Non-Muslim worlds, Muslim media is always blamed as biased and unreliable by the Western news agencies. This situation promotes distrust between the Muslim and the Non-Muslim worlds.

8

The Twenty-first Century - Prospects for the Muslim World

The twentieth century is over and it seems a particularly pertinent time to assess the achievements of the Muslim World throughout that century. The arrival of the twentieth century saw Western colonisers at the peak of their power, a power based on their control of industrial development. Britain was the largest colonial power in the world and controlled many parts of the Muslim World including the important sea routes. A new era was heralded in the middle of the century with most Muslim countries gaining independence from their colonial rulers. New hopes emerged with independence and the period was characterised by an upsurge in Islamic revivalism. This revival gained ground and quickly spread all over the Muslim World. The current politico-economic development, the search for means to extend cooperation among Muslim countries, the establishment of the OIC and its other subsidiaries such as the Islamic Development Bank, the Islamic Chamber of Commerce and Industry, and the International Islamic Universities, can all trace their roots to this revival.

This chapter focuses mainly on the possible ways and means with which to improve the overall state of development in the

Muslim World. However, before proceeding further, it seems imperative to review the current process of globalisation in the context of discussions made in previous chapters. The outcome of the analysis of this study reflects the poor state of development in the Muslim World in comparison to the Non-Muslim World. It is generally believed that the cause of this inequality is the prevalence of widespread poverty and illiteracy in the Muslim World. However, this is not essentially true, as the major obstacles to the development of the Muslim World have been highlighted as: the high and increasing burden of foreign debt, the lack of competence in global trade and foreign investment, regional conflicts and high defence expenditures, and the interference of Western dominated political interests. Allied to these problems is also the fact that Western based technology and media are used as efficient tools with which to further oppress the Muslim World and retard its progress. Moreover, as mentioned in chapter two, the population growth rate of Muslim countries is higher than that of Non-Muslim countries, which suggests that if the present trends continue, the development gap between the Muslim and the Non-Muslim Worlds will continue to widen throughout this century. This situation demands that Muslim countries think urgently about their role in the contemporary globalisation process before this gap becomes too wide to bridge.

Globalisation or Recolonisation?

It is evident from the present analysis that the nature of contemporary globalisation did not emerge as a 'natural' development but rather as a created entity driven by the major global players through agencies, such as the IMF, the World Bank, WTO and the global media. The obvious objective of all these organisations and their activities is to control the entire world, particularly the Muslim World, economically, politically, culturally, ideologically and militarily. This process can be defined by the following diagram.

Globalisation and its Mechanism of Control

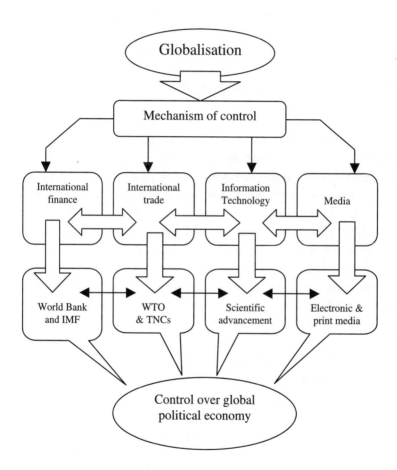

Chapter one focused mainly on conceptual issues, and discussed the various theories pertaining to the globalisation issue. It argued that globalisation is a process causing the 'interdependence' of countries and their economies. The discussion in the subsequent chapters, based on current facts and figures, reflect the fact that globalisation is not only a matter of interdependence, but also includes elements of 'dependence' where one group of countries is totally reliant on another group. In essence, this divides countries into two groups, 'developed' and 'developing', or in other words, the First World and the Third World. In the globalisation process, the position of 'interdependence' may be attributed to the developed world, whereas for the developing world 'dependence' is more the norm.

It is obvious from the analysis of the previous chapters that the Muslim World is lagging far behind the developing world in the overall field of socio-economic development. Therefore, it can safely be said that dependency is a truer fact of life in the Muslim World than the 'developing Non-Muslim World'. However, this is not a simple and straightforward process as it incorporates a series of inter-connected activities that have an effect on international finance, foreign trade, technology, international politics, media, culture and even ideologies. In such a context we must begin to search for a new definition of globalisation, i.e.:

> The world-wide phenomenon, globalisation is a composition of a series of processes of domination through global political economy, including international finance and trade, informational technologies, media, international defence and strategic issues. In other words; it is systematised process of making and breaking of countries, imposing ideologies and programmes of one, or a group of countries, over others. Within the First World, globalisation is the integration of economies, which promotes economies of scale. In the context

of the First and the Third worlds, it promotes dependence of the latter on the former. However, with regard to the Muslim World, it is characterised by 'dependence' as well as the imposition of alien ideologies. In current global affairs, this whole exercise of globalisation has accelerated the process of dominance by the First World.

How is the present process of globalisation different from the process of colonisation? The answer is simple. During colonisation, colonisers kept themselves in power mainly on the basis of their military power. In the era of globalisation the same colonisers are once again evident but this time their hold on power in based mainly on their control of global finance, trade, politics, media and advancements in science and technology. Therefore, despite the fact that the present process of globalisation looks like the outgrowth of neo-colonialism; in reality it is a process of 'recolonisation'. However, whether it is colonisation, globalisation or recolonisation, one fact remains true, the colonisers and the colonised are still the same. The only thing which has changed is that the 'gap' between the 'rich and poor', and the 'have and have nots' has increased many times more.

This entire discussion is summarised by the following diagram and highlights the current situation of the increased dependence of Third World countries on the First World. It is important to mention here that, the situation of the Muslim World, which can be considered the 'Fourth World', is different to that of the Third World. In spite of having a sufficient supply of resources (including financial and human), the dependence of the Muslim World on the First World has reached the level of oppression. The socio-economic and political situation of the Muslim World discussed in previous chapters clearly attests to this fact.

The Muslim World and the Recolonisation
Process in the Twenty-first Century

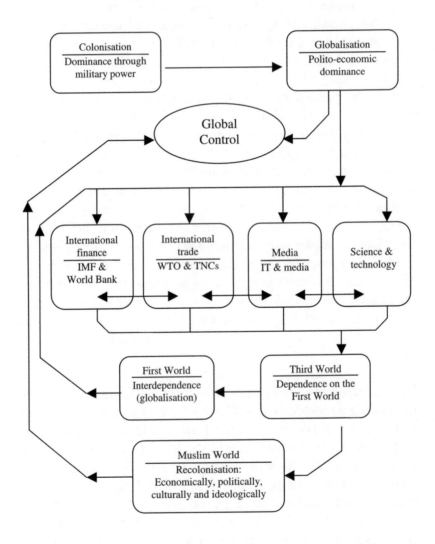

Islamic Approach to Globalisation

According to Muslim belief, Islam is a complete code for all aspects of life. However, during the colonial period most Muslim countries blindly followed Western economic models where the main emphasis was placed on growth rather than the concept of fair distribution. These models were directed by Western institutions whose real objective was to develop Muslim countries as a source of cheap raw materials for import. Presently, the 'exports to the Western countries have been pursued with such vigour that Muslim countries have become marginalised with regard to trade between themselves. The pursuit of economic growth has made the Muslim countries subservient to, and trapped by, its technological and financial dependency on the West to an extent hitherto unseen' (Choudhury, 1998:196).

The Islamic approach to globalisation is presented in the following paragraphs and it stresses the need for cooperation among Muslim countries leading to their politico-economic integration. However, the reality of the situation is that, unfortunately, the status and position of the Muslim World is declining day-by-day. If the present trends of decline and recolonisation continue at their present rate, the Muslim World will face an extremely critical situation over the next few decades. What it in fact amounts to is a question of survival, and Muslim countries must realise that they have to take measures to protect themselves if they are not to become totally excluded from global affairs. This struggle for existence has to be conducted in several areas, i.e., the development and strengthening of the Islamic financial system, promotion of mutual trade, cooperation in the fields of science and technology, media and information, and most importantly of all, the creation of a system of common security.

The key to the success of this whole programme lies with economic motives. It is therefore necessary that these countries seek to encourage the promotion of mutual trade through institutions such as the OIC and the Islamic Development Bank. This increase in cooperation will lead to a further promotion of mutual confidence within the entire Muslim World. The step-by-step nature of this development programme will enable them to solve their problems without external interference. Indeed, a true measure of the success of these proposals would be the emergence of a situation where the Muslim World is able to intervene in an effective and meaningful way in solving various crises in other parts of the world. Such a development would be beneficial in maintaining the balance of power in global affairs, as well as in helping to reduce the burden on the United Nations, which could then afford to focus more of its attention on developmental issues rather than political disputes.

However, in order to achieve such a position, the Muslim World has to strengthen various institutions, such as the Islamic Development Bank (IDB), Islamic Chamber of Commerce, Industry and Commodity Exchange (ICCI&CE), Islamic Centre for the Development of Trade (ICDT), Islamic Foundation for Science, Technology and Development (IFSTAD) and in particular, the Islamic media and news agencies, that already exist. In addition, they also need to establish new institutions for the protection of their own interests such as the Muslim Monitory Fund (MMF), Human Development Fund (HDF), Islamic Security Council (ISC), and Islamic Defence Force (IDF). The following diagram and discussion illustrate the blueprint for this proposed model.

A Suggestive Model for Islamic Approach to Globalisation

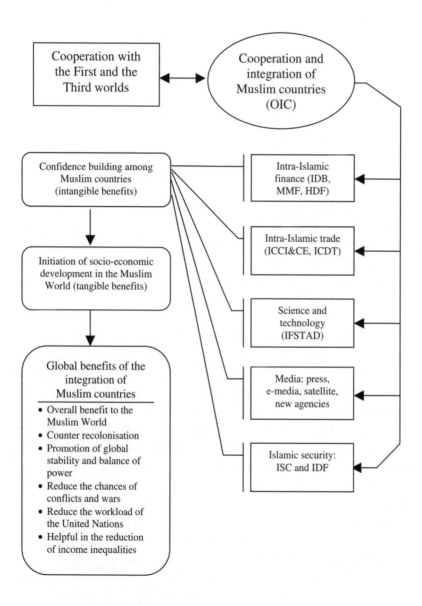

An Agenda for the Twenty-first Century

It should be noted that the current globalisation trend and the state of underdevelopment in the Muslim World are interrelated issues that demand urgent attention. Furthermore, unless the ruling elite in Muslim countries realise the severity of their problems, and undertake a genuine political commitment to solving them, their current situation will become dramatically worse. The Muslim World requires structured and comprehensive planning for the future of the Muslim *Ummah*. A number of short, medium and long-term strategies need to be adopted for this purpose. These strategies should then be placed within a specified operational timeframe: period one; 2005-2015, period two; 2016-2030, and period three; 2031-2050. The period from now until 2005 should be utilised for mutual consultation in order to establish consensus and political commitment. The whole process is built on the need to establish new institutions, as well as strengthening existing ones, within the Muslim World.

One of the key issues determining the success of this strategy lies in the performance of the OIC. There exists no other organisation in the world where such a large number of countries have joined together solely on the basis of religion. Despite the weakness of this organisation, it still provides the best basis for all future development activities in the Muslim World. Therefore, the steps discussed in the following paragraphs should be pursued through the OIC, the Muslim World has no other or better alternative. In the context of the contemporary global environment, any future cooperation among Muslim countries needs to be predicated on economic factors, otherwise it is doomed to failure. With regard to the above stated approach to Islamic globalisation, 'period one' - 2005-2015 (i.e., the short-term strategy), requires Muslim countries to make efforts on at least five important fronts:

- Establishment of a sound central financial system for the Muslim World
- Common Islamic market for the promotion of mutual trade
- Advancement in the fields of science and technology
- Well established media and news agencies
- Establishment of the ISC and the IDF

Despite eight years of devastating war between Iran and Iraq, the Gulf War and the continuing conflict in Afghanistan, the leaders of the Muslim World have proved unable to resolve conflicts amongst themselves. The Iran-Iraq war came to an end in August 1998 through the efforts of the UN Security Council but the war in Afghanistan continues to rage. It seems that the leaders of the Muslim World are at a loss as to how to resolve their problems. The proposed project for Islamic global cooperation may go some way towards suggesting a possible solution to this state of affairs. It is still difficult to comprehend the extent to which the leaders of the Muslim countries respect the art of negotiation and the dialogue between themselves. There is an enormous potential for international trade between Muslim countries and significant research has already been conducted on various aspects of economic cooperation.

Now is the time for Muslim countries to realise that they must develop their own markets and not merely be used as a dumping ground for second-rate goods and services from the Western industrial countries. First, they should focus on regional and sub-regional economic unions, e.g., Arab Common Market, Arab Maghreb Union, The Gulf Cooperation Council and Economic Cooperation Organisation, etc. When this cooperation is sufficiently strengthened, the next step should be inter-cooperation between the regional economic groups leading to the development of a fully-fledged 'Islamic common market'. This task is not difficult to achieve as the compact geographical position of the Muslim countries gives them a comparative advantage over trade with Western industrial countries. Furthermore, the cost of transportation will be far lower in Intra-*Ummatic* trade as compared to trade with Australia, American or the European Union. Moreover, due to the fact that they are all developing countries, their cost of production is also much lower than that of the Western world, which means that they accrue additional advantages arising from economies of scale.

However, to achieve this objective, there is an urgent need to strengthen the Islamic Centre for the Development of Trade, the Islamic Chamber of Commerce, Industry and Commodity Exchange, and the Islamic Shipowners Association. These institutions are already established for this purpose and are working under the administrative control of the OIC. The role of the Islamic Chamber of Commerce is of particular importance as this institution is composed of the federations of chambers of commerce and industry or national chambers, and other similar institutions existing in Muslim countries. This indicates that this institution is crucial in providing a strong foundation for promoting trade within the Muslim World.

As indicated earlier, the Muslim World is under huge financial strain from the crippling burden of foreign debts, particularly those of the IMF and the World Bank. At present the situation is that both these global money-lending institutions are receiving a huge amount of interest on the loans which they have advanced to many countries. The amount received as interest is utilised to advance further loans to countries so that they can pay back their interest or in certain cases just keep them going. There are some countries that have repaid more interest than the total amount of the initial loan. Under current global circumstances there is no way-out from this vicious circle. The ruling authorities of the Muslim countries need to develop a positive strategy in order to redress this alarming situation. To do this requires strengthening the Islamic Development Bank so as to enable it to eliminate the dictatorial role of the IMF and the World Bank.

The ruling families of several Muslim countries have large amounts of financial reserves and investments in Western banks and stock exchanges. It is essential that a significant part of this money be taken and invested through the Islamic Development Bank. Furthermore, a Muslim Monetary Fund (MMF) should be established with its primary objective to remove Muslim countries from the vicious circle of foreign debt. This action would drastically reduce the financial burden on the annual budgets of these countries, thus enabling more resources to be diverted to tackling issues such as poverty. It would also enable them to initiate various industrial projects, which would generate income and employment opportunities.

In addition to the MMF, the Muslim World also needs to establish a Human Development Fund (HDF). At the initial stage, this money should be utilised to establish a basic infrastructural network and to start various human development projects in deprived communities throughout the various Muslim countries. In this instance, the Islamic Development Bank would not only be a key institution in improving the financial condition of Muslim countries, but also a means of enhancing intra-Islamic trade, as well as helping in the research and development of science, technology, Muslim media and other projects, with a view to eliminating mass poverty.

It does not need to be emphasised further that the Muslim World is lagging behind the rest of the world in the field of science and technology. The same is also true of the media. In both these fields the Muslim World is totally dependent upon the West. This is one of the main reasons as to why the Muslim countries have no voice and weightage in global affairs. As discussed previously, there are various institutions already working in this area under the auspices of the OIC, e.g, International Islamic News Agency, Islamic States Broadcasting Organisation, and the Islamic Foundation for Science, Technology and Development. The problem is that the limited spectrum of the activities of these institutions has made them completely ineffective. Muslim countries must begin to establish common news agencies of the level of the BBC, Voice of America or CNN. This undertaking requires an availability of satellites in space (Syed, 1997:183-211). Some Muslim countries have gained the necessary technological skills in this area but are unable to launch a programme due to financial constraints. However, this hurdle can be removed by initiating joint-ventures with the rich Muslim countries who do not possess such skills. This programme would constitute a huge advance for the Muslim media, and is essential if it is to assume a leading role in global affairs. These efforts will not only help to project the Islamic cause in the world but will also help the Western world to better understand the Muslim World. Towards this end it may be expedient for regions to develop their own media policies as a first step towards a more comprehensive and integrated policy for the Muslim World as a whole. This would require establishing a team of experts for the purposes of creating the desired impact and maintaining an overall harmony and balance in the projection of themes and ideas. The Muslim media must embark upon a campaign of truth to impress upon the world that the cause of peace in the world is achievable through cooperation and communication.

As discussed in chapter five, in a rapidly changing world, the concept of security has become much broader and refined in shape, encompassing not just military power but also local, regional, political and economic issues. Despite the prevalence of widespread poverty, illiteracy, hunger and debt burden, Muslim countries are forced to allocate a significant chunk of their financial resources to the defence sector, due to the internal and external threats to their security. It is estimated that at present they spend around 77 billion US dollars on defence and that nearly six million people are currently employed in this sector of the economy (IISS, 1999:300-04). Through a system of mutual cooperation, a large amount of these financial and human resources can be saved and utilised in other productive sectors of the economy.

Several Muslim countries have, and are continuing to face the problems of internal instability, conflict and war. The Palestine crises, the Iran-Iraq war, the Gulf war, Afghanistan, Kashmir, Sudan, Western Sahara, Indonesia and East Timor are all clear and real examples of these problems. These events show an obvious and urgent need for the creation of an Islamic Security Council (ISC). This council should have two objectives. Firstly, on the political front, it should be the supreme authority for dealing with internal and external conflicts in the Muslim World. Secondly, it should be the governing authority of a joint Islamic Defence Force (IDF) to respond to any aggression by a member state. The question is, how to establish this force? A first step would be a unilateral agreement to begin cutting defence budgets by one percent starting in 2005, eventually rising to 10 percent by 2015. This reduction would save more than US$42 billion (IISS, 1999:300-04). Some of this money could be utilised to expand the activities of the Islamic Development Bank while the rest could be used to establish the IDF. The overall strength of the IDF should be not be less than one million personnel. The IDF can play an effective NATO type role in preventing internal or external threats to the Muslim World. The advantages in establishing the IDF will be multifarious and not solely limited to security issues. It will give Muslim countries the confidence and the means with which to solve their own problem rather than constantly having to depend upon the major global players. With the passage of time, the IDF will be useful in tackling the unjust monopoly of Western countries and in maintaining a balance of power in global affairs. It is hoped that with the establishment and existence of the IDF, problems such as the Iran-Iraq war, the Gulf war, the occupation on Palestine and Al-Quds will not happen in the future.

Another point of primary importance is the imbalance of power within the UN Security Council, which sees five permanent members enjoy an undue and unjust monopoly in world affairs. Recently, a number of other countries (particularly India which has never accepted any of the UN resolutions with regard to the right of Kashmiris to self-determination) have been very active in attempting to secure a permanent seat on the UN Security Council. Muslim countries must also try to secure at least one permanent seat on this Council. This seat should be jointly operated through the OIC. It is important that with regard to this whole proposed programme, the above mentioned activities have to be completed within the time frame set out in 'period-one' (2005-2015). When these proposals has been established on a sound footing, further measures can then be undertaken in 'period-two' (2016-2030). During this period, steps should be taken to merge the economies and political activities of Muslim countries based on the pattern of the European Union. By the end of this fifteen-year period:

- There should be a single currency for OIC member countries
- Establishment of various joint Islamic industrial, commercial, saving and agricultural development banks
- The IDF should have been established as a single joint defence force for the whole Muslim World
- Poverty and the debt burden should be eliminated
- By strengthening the OIC, the status, role and authority of the head of this institution should become more than a formal Secretary General

- By the completion of these objectives, this transitional period should lead to the establishment of a foundation for the overall industrialisation and integration of Islamic countries

After the completion of the above steps, the third and final phase (2031-2050) should be to complete the process of unification, ending with the establishment of the 'United States of Islam' (USI). The strategy of unification should be adopted in such a way that at the apex level, there should be a loose federation of member states. By keeping sufficient internal autonomy, all Muslim countries would remain independent in their internal affairs while the four major sectors, i.e., currency, defence, foreign affairs and communication would be under the control of a 'federal-body'. This would provide enormous politio-economic benefits to those living in the Muslim World. By the end of this stage (2050), the OIC should be converted into a 'federal governing body' of the Muslim World and the position of present Secretary General should be changed to a formal Caliph. This federation of Muslim countries should be based on democratic principles. However, much exercise and research is needed to make this framework compatible with the requirements of the modern age without reverting to a medieval-style government.

A Dream or Reality?

Under the contemporary global environment, and due to the declining state of the Muslim World, the above proposal does not seem much more than a dream. However, if it is a dream, it is the dream of the masses of the Muslim World from East Asia to West Africa, and history suggests that dreams have the potential to become reality. Two centuries ago, who would have thought that more than four-dozen North American states would be united into one single country eventually becoming a super power in world affairs? A century ago, did anyone imagine that the European states, which have completely separate cultures, languages, state systems, and a long history of conflict and war, would succeed in establishing a progressive union? More recently, who would have thought that Soviet Union, a huge nuclear super-power would be defeated by an extremely poor country like Afghanistan and later, disintegrate into several parts? Muslim countries possess almost 1400 years of common history and the Prophet Muhammad elaborated a comprehensive system of law for government and international relations. Now in the twenty-first century the question remains as to why Muslim countries have not been able to thus far establish a practical and operational union acting according to their own interests and needs along the lines of multilateral institutions such as the EU and G-7?

When considering the process of the formation of a 'union', Muslim countries have an added advantage over their North American and European counterparts in that they share a common culture, common history, common belief and above all a widespread desire for this integration at the grassroots level. Deriving strength from its rich tradition and past, this proposed union has the potential to set an example to the rest of the world. Therefore, appropriate strategies need to be developed in order for this dream to materialise. The ruling classes of the Muslim countries must realise that, rather than begging from others, self-sufficiency and self-reliance hold the prospects for the future development and improvement of all. Sadly, the present position and desire of the Muslim ruling classes to undertake such a project does not look promising as can be judged from the text from a renowned Western journal. The London based weekly *Economist* (13 November 1999) writes: 'Turkey's Islamists Recai Kutan, leader of Turkey's Islamic Virtue Party, condemned the killing in a bomb attack last month of a prominent pro-secular academic, Ahmet Taner Kislali, some angry onlookers shouted: 'Shut up and go to Iran.' A modified Mr Kutan beat a hasty retreat. He knows that Turkey's Islamists are still seen by many Turks as a threat to the secular state founded by Kemal Ataturk 76 years ago. Mr Kutan, an avuncular septuagenarian, wants to persuade these Turks that they are wrong. He has been Virtue's leader since it took the place of another Islamist party, Welfare, which was ejected from government under pressure from Turkey's generals in 1997. Last week Mr Kutan was in Washington meeting American officials and Jewish groups. He sought to persuade them that the call by Islamists for Turkey's withdrawal from NATO and for the establishment of an 'Islamic common market' were things of the past. If Virtue were allowed to be elected to power, it would be their 'best and most reliable friend'.

This quotation does not need any explanation except to repeat the above stated fact that if the rulers of the Muslim World realised the aspirations of their own people, they need not beg power from others. They have to understand that in the long run the unity of the Muslim World is also in the interests of their own descendants. Is it not worth seeking affiliation with your own people rather than looking elsewhere? These rulers must realise that they should listen to their people and keep in contact with them, as they are the source of their real power, not 'American officials' or 'Jewish groups'.

A careful consideration of this approach indicates that not only is unity among Muslim countries essential but it is also important in promoting an effective role for the Muslim World in global affairs. The call for mutual cooperation is therefore composed of two components; internal and external. The internal component is unity within the Muslim World while the external component refers to its relations with the outside world. The contemporary global situation demands a rational interpretation of Islam in tandem with the mobilisation of political power in the Muslim World. This fact needs to be highlighted so that Islam does not prohibit Muslims from working with the Western world on matters of common interest. Thus efforts should be made to promote mutual trust between the Muslim and the Non-Muslim Worlds. Muslim countries must try to avoid confrontation with the West. They must evolve and reshape their policies in a manner that seeks to promote a spirit of mutual understanding and goodwill. This is a very challenging task but they must accomplish it, it is essential to their future survival. Areas of convergence need to be emphasised and carefully worked-upon in a bid to establish better relations, whereas the areas of divergence need to be seriously and meaningfully dealt with, in order to defuse tension. These activities will not only serve the interests of the Muslim World but will also prove beneficial to the promotion of global stability, peace and prosperity.

Choudhury (1998:204) has argued that each Muslim country must take a leading role and initiate the process of restructuring its own system by linking itself with international politico-economic changes in the Muslim World. In his view, such actions can help to generate a framework of inter-relations within, and between, Muslim countries that can then be broadened out to the global level. A careful consideration of this strategy indicates that it relies mostly upon government initiatives while the experience of the past decades shows that those in power in Muslim countries have generally put their own personal interests first and have proved incapable of taking such big steps. In the present age of democratisation, any feasible approach to reform should be generated from the grassroots level.

In order to accomplish these undertakings, two simultaneous approaches in the internal and external sectors need to be adopted. The most important step with regard to the internal sector is the need for collaboration between the general public, liberal and moderate Muslim intellectuals and politicians, with a view to establishing pressure groups and gaining public support within the country, in order to eliminate social evils. At the *Ummatic* level, such national movements should work together in close coordination so as to affect the maximum influence on the governments of Muslim countries. They need to put moral and political pressure on their own respective governments to promote coordination among the Muslim countries. The objective of this approach ought not to be to bring about a revolution within the Muslim World, which may lead to a disaster; rather it should start as a peaceful and social evolutionary process starting from the grassroots level up. Such efforts in various Muslim countries would be helpful in creating internal solidarity and stability, as well as external coordination and harmony at the *Ummatic* level. This process if properly implemented could result in the idea of 'Islamic globalisation' becoming a functioning system where the Muslim World can gradually begin to solve its own problems.

Bibliography

Abdullah, Daud A. in Ahmad Sidqui al Dajani (translated from the Arabic by Daud A. Abdullah) (1997), *Britain's Obligations Towards the Arabs Concerning Palestine*, London: The Palestinian Return Centre.

Abu-Rabi, Ibrahim M. (ed.) (1995) *Islamic Resurgence: Challenges, Directions & Future Perspectives – A Round Table with Professor Khurshid Ahmad*, Islamabad: Institute of Policy Studies.

Aburish, Said K. (1998), *A Brutal Friendship: The West and the Arab Elite*, London: Indigo.

AbuSulayman, AbdulHamid A. (1994), *Towards an Islamic Theory of International Relations – New Directions for Methodology and Though*, Herndon: The International Institute of Islamic Thought.

Addleton, Jonathan S. (1992), *Undermining the Centre – The Gulf Migration and Pakistan*, Karachi: Oxford University Press.

Aglionby, John (March 7, 2000), *Guardian* (The Daily).

Ahmad, Etazaz (1996), 'Capital Inflow and National Debt', *The Pakistan Development Review*, Vol. 35-4, Part-II.

Ahmad, Ishtiaq (1991), *The Concept of an Islamic State in Pakistan – An Analysis of Ideological Controversies*, Lahore: Vanguard.

Ahmad, Khurshid (1986), *Studies in Islamic Economics*, Jeddah: International Centre for Islamic Research in Islamic Economic.

Ahmad, Khurshid (1994), *Islamic Approach to Development: Some Policy Implications*, Islamabad: Institute of Policy Studies.

Ahmad, Khurshid (1995), 'Islam and the New World Order' in S.M. Koreshi, *Western Fundamentalism in Action – New World Order*, Islamabad: Institute of Policy Studies.

Ahmad, Khurshid (ed.) (1976), *Studies in Islamic Economics*, Jeddah: International Centre for Research in Islamic Economics.

Ahmad, S. Akbar (1999), *Islam Today: A Short Introduction to the Muslim World,* London: I.B. Tauris & Co. Ltd.

Ahmad, Salman (1995), *A General Equilibrium Model of Custom Unions Among Islamic Countries*, Islamabad: International Islamic University.

Ahmad, Sultan (2 March, 2000) 'Ill Effects of Globalisation', *Dawn – Internet Edition*, [http://www.dawn.com].

Ahmad, Ziauddin (1991), *Islam, Poverty and Income Distribution*, Leicester: The Islamic Foundation.

Ahmed, Abd El Rahman Yousf (1991), *The Steps for Islamic Economic Integration in Contemporary Circumstances* (A paper presented in the International Symposium on the Islamic Common Market), Cairo: El-Azhar University.

Ahmed, Shaikh Mansoor (8 August 2000), 'Globalisation Under Attack', *Dawn – Internet Edition* [http://www.dawn.com].

Ahmed, Viqar and Rashid Amjad (1984), *The Management of Pakistan's Economy 1947-82*, Karachi: Oxford University Press.

Ahsan, Abdullah al (1988) *OIC – The Organisation of the Islamic Conference*, Herndon: The International Institute of Islamic Thought.

Ahsan, Abdullah al (1992), *Ummah or Nation? Identity Crises in Contemporary Muslim Society,* Leicester: The Islamic Foundation.

Ahsan, Muhammad (1994), 'Theories of Migration with Particular Reference to Islam and Pakistan', *The Islamic Quarterly,* Vol. XXXVIII-3.

Ahsan, Muhammad (1999), 'Education: The Twenty-first Century and the Human Development in the Muslim World,' *Muslim Education Quarterly*, Vol. 16-3.

Ahsan, Muhammad (February 1999), 'Human Development Strategies of the Muslim World: A Multi-Dimensional Approach,' *National Development and Security – A Quarterly Journal*, Vol. VII-3.

Akhbar-e-Watan (March 2000), Vol. 31-3, London.

Ali, Asghar (1987), *The Origin and Development of Islam*, London: Sangam Books Ltd.

Ali, Syed Akbar (November 1999), 'Towards Nuclear Safe South Asia: Options, Choices and Constraints for Paksitan', *National Development and Security – Quarterly Journal*, Vol. VIII-2.

Amandurdyev, A.N. (1998), 'Internal and External Regional Cooperation for Peace and Development', in S.M. Rehman (ed.), *Central Asia – Regional*

Cooperation for Peace and Development, Rawalpindi: Foundation for Research on International Environment National Development and Security.

Amin, Tahir (1995), *Mass Resistance in Kashmir*, Islamabad: Institute of Policy Studies.

Amnesty – Human Rights Worldwide, Vol. 103, September-October, 2000.

Amnesty International (May 2000), [http:// www. amnesty. org/.../sudan?].

Amnesty International, *Amnesty Report on Burma – Human Rights Still Denied* (internet edition) November, 1994. [http:// www. falcon. cc.ukans. edu/~jrchien/ politics/ amnesty 94.html].

Arberry, A.J. (ed) (1969), *Religion in the Middle East*, Cambridge: Cambridge University Press.

Armstrong, Karen (27 May 2000), 'The West is Still Demonising Islam', *Times Weekend*.

Arnove, Anthony, 'Introduction', in Anthony Arnove (ed.) (2000) *Iraq Under Siege – The Deadly Impact of Sanctions and War*, London: Pluto Press.

Asghar, Sadiq Mehmood (1989), *The History of South Asia*, Karachi: Adara-i-Adabyat.

Aziz, Mir Abdul (1998), *Fifty Years Saga of Kashmir Struggle and Prospects for Peace*, Karachi: Sangam.

Badeau, John S. (1968), *The American Approach to the Arab World*, New York: Harper and Row Publishers.

Baker, William W. (1994), *Kashmir – Happy Valley, Valley of Death*, Las Vegas: Defenders Publications.

Bandow, Dough and Ian Vasquez (eds.) (1994), *Perpetuating Poverty: The World Bank, the IMF and the Developing World*, Washington D.C.: CATO Institute.

Bannock, Grahm (1992), in R.E. Baxter and Evan Davis, *Dictionary of Economics*, London: Penguin Books Ltd.

Bashar, Abdul Mannan (1999), *Economy, Trade and Social Development*, Dhaka: Sagu Co.

Beg, Aslam Mirza (1998), 'Strategic Management of Geopolitical and Geoeconomic Interests in Central Asian Region', in S.M. Rehaman (ed.)

(1998), *Central Asia: Regional Cooperation for Peace and Development*, Rawalpindi: Foundation for Research on International Environment National Development and Security.

Beg, Mirza Aslam (1994), *Development and Security: Thoughts and Reflections*, Rawalpindi: Foundation for Research on International Environment National Development and Security.

Beg, Mirza Aslam (1999), *National Security: Diplomacy and Defence*, Rawalpindi: Foundation for Research on International Environment National Development and Security.

Beinin, Joel and Joe Stork (1996), *Political Islam: A Reader*, London: I.B. Tauris & Co. Ltd.

Bellah, Robert (1970), 'Religious Evolution', in *Beyond Belief: Essays on Religion in a Post-Traditional World*, New York: Harper and Row.

Berger, Peter L. (1967), *The Scared Canopy: Elements of Sociological Theory of Religion*, Garden City: Doubleday.

Berger, Peter L. (1967), *The Scared Canopy: Elements of Sociological Theory of Religion*, Garden City: Doubleday.

Beyer, Peter F. (1996), 'Privatization and the Public Influence of Religion in Global Society', in Mike Featherstone (ed) *Global Culture: Nationalism, Globalization and Modernity*, London: SAGE Publications Ltd.

Bhuyan, Ayubur Rahman *et. al.* (eds.) (1996), *Towards an Islamic Common Market, Proceedings of the International Seminar on Islamic Common Market held during December 18-20, 1993*, Dhaka: Islamic Economic Research Bureau.

Boisard, Marcel (1986), *Humanism in Islam*, Indianapolis: America Trust Publications.

Brown, Mark Malloch, in UNDP (1999), *Human Development Report 1999*, New York: Oxford University Press.

Brunell, Peter (1997), *Foreign Aid in a Changing World*, Buckingham: Open University Press.

Castello-Cortes, Ian, *et. al.,* (eds.) (editions: 1994, 1995, 1998 and 1999), *World Reference Atlas*, London: Dorling Kindersley Ltd.

Caufield, Catherine (1998), *Master of Illusion – The World Bank and the Poverty of Nations*, London: Macmillan Publishers Ltd.

Centre for Research and Studies on Kuwait (1996), *Iraqi Aggression on Kuwait – The Truth and the Tragedy*, Kuwait: Centre for Research and Studies on Kuwait.

Chapra, M. Umar (1992), *Islam and the Economic Challenges*, Leicester: The Islamic Foundation.

Chapra, M. Umar (2000), 'Why has Islam Prohibited Interest? Rationale Behind the Prohibition of Interest', *Review of Islamic Economics*, Vol. 9-2000, Journal of International Association for Islamic Economics and the Islamic Foundation.

Charles, Prince (A lecture delivered on 27 October, 1993, at Oxford University), quoted in S.M. Koreshi, *New World Order: Western Fundamentalism in Action*, Islamabad: Institute of Policy Studies, 1995.

Chossudovsky, Michel (1998), *The Globalisation of Poverty – Impact of IMF and World Bank Reforms*, London: Zed Books Ltd.

Choudhury, Masudul Alam (1998), *Studies in Islamic Social Sciences*, London: Macmillan Press Ltd.

CIA (July 2000), *World Fact Book 1999*, [http://www. odci. gov/ cia/ publications/ factbook].

Cindourki, Sadi (Jan.-April 1992), 'Economic Cooperation Among OIC Countries and the Islamic Common Market', *Journal of Economic Cooperation Among Islamic Countries,* Vol. 13-1,2.

Cohen, Avner (2000), *Israel and the Bomb*, Columbia University Press.

Conciliation Commission for Palestine, *Report of the United Nations Economic Survey Mission,* New York: United Nations Document A/AC.25/6, p. 9, cited in *CAABU*, Vol. 4: (Council for the Advancement of Arab-British Understanding, London).

Cooper, John, Muhammad Mahmud and Ron Nettler (eds.) (1998), *Islam and Modernity – Muslim Intellectuals Respond,* London: I.B. Tauris & Co. Ltd.

Coote, Blinda and Caroline LeQuesne (1996), *The Trade Trap: Poverty and the Global Commodity Market*, Oxford: Oxfam.

Cowasjee, Ardeshir (23 July 2000), *Dawn – Internet Edition*, [http://www.dawn.com].

Cox, Robert W. (1993), 'Structural Issues of Global Governance: Implications for Europe,' in Stephen Gill (ed.), *Gramsci's Historical Materialism and International Relations,* Cambridge: Cambridge University Press.

Cragg, Kenneth (1980), *Islam from Within – Anthology of a Religion,* Balmount: Wadsworth Publishing Company.

Cragg, Kenneth (1988), *The House of Islam,* Balmount: Wadsworth Publishing Company.

Dar, Naeem (ed.) (1999), *Muslim Directory,* London: Blackmore Press.

Dasgupta, Biplab (1998), *Structural Adjustment, Global Trade and the New Political Economy of Development,* London: Zed Books.

Dawn – Internet Edition (The Daily) (various issues), [http:// www. dawn. com].

East Timor (May 2000), [http://www.law.qub.ac.uk].

Economist (The Weekly) (various issues), London.

Economist Intelligence Unit (1999 and 2000) (various country reports), London.

Elliott, Larry (4 December 1999), 'Secret Talks – Key Decisions were made in Private by the Big Players', *Guardian* (The Daily).

Ernst, Carl W. (15 July 2000), *Dawn – Internet Edition,* [http:// www. dawn.com].

Esposito, John L., (ed.) (1995), *The Oxford Encyclopaedia of the Modern Islamic World* (Vol. 3), New York: Oxford University Press.

Farhat, Seema (1996), 'Globalisation, Information Technology, and Economic Development', *The Pakistan Development Review,* Vol. 35-4, Winter.

Farooq, Shakweer, 'Prospects for the Establishment of the Islamic Common Market and the Role of the Islamic Development Bank', in Ayubur Rahman Bhuyan, *Towards An Islamic Common Market,* Dhaka: Islamic Economic Research Bureau.

Farzin, Hossein, (January 1991), 'Food Aid: Positive and Negative Effects in Somalia', *The Journal of Developing Areas.*

Featherstone, Mike (1996), 'Global Culture: An Introduction', in Mike Featherstone (ed) *Global Culture: Nationalism, Globalisation and Modernity,* London: SAGE Publications Ltd.

168

Federation of American Scientists (24 August 2000), *Israel – Nuclear Weapons* [http:// www. fas.org/ nuke/guide/ israel/ nuke/index. html].

Finger, J. Michael (1994), 'The High Cost of Trade Protectionism to the Third World', in Doug Bandow and Ian Vásquez (eds.) *Perpetuating Poverty – The World Bank, the IMF and the Developing World*, Washington D.C.: CATO Institute.

Fisk, Robert, (3 November 1999) 'The West's Fear of Islam Is No Excuse for Racism', *The Independent* (The Daily).

Forbes Magazine (1999), 'The World's Richest People' (6 July 1998), cited in UNDP, *Human Development Report 1999*, New York: Oxford University Press.

Fraser, T.G. (1995), *The Arab-Israeli Conflict*, London: Macmillan Press Ltd.

Freeland, Jonathan (1 December 1999), 'Powerless People', *Guardian* (The Daily).

Gabb, Sean (ed.) (1998), *American Claims About the Al-Shifa Factory Put to the Test*, London: The Sudan Foundation.

Galbraith, J.K. and Nicole Salinger (1990), *Almost Everyone's Guide to Economics*, London: Penguine Books.

Gauhar, Altaf (ed.) (1978), *The Challenge of Islam*, London: Islamic Council of Europe.

George, Susan (1990), *A Fate Worse Than Debt: World Financial Crisis and the Poor*, New York: Grove Weidenfeld.

George, Susan (4 December 1999), 'Festival of Ideas Outside WTO – The Battle Over Trade', *Guardian* (The Daily).

Ghazali, Abdus Sattar (8 April 2000), *Dawn – Internet Edition*, [http:// www.dawn.com].

Giddens, Anthony (1998), *The Third Way: The Renewal of Social Democracy*, Cambridge: Polity Press.

Gilani, Amir Akbar (1998), *International Trade and the Islamic Common Market*, New York: Wada Press.

Guardian (The Daily) (various issues).

Gust, Robert (26 June 1999) 'How to Make Aid Works', *Economist* (The Weekly).

Habibi, Habib Ullah (1967), *Education and National Development*, New York, J.L. Publishers.

Haeri, Shaykh Fadhlalla (1993), *The Elements of Islam,* Dorset: Element Books Ltd.

Haider, S.M. (ed.) (1994), *Pakistan, Central Asia and the Region – Prospects for Regional Cooperation*, Lahore: Progressive Publishers.

Halliday, Denis J. (1999), 'Iraq and the UN's Weapon of Mass Destruction', in M. Simon Baker, *National and International Affairs*, New York: Rivermead.

Hansen-Kuhn, Karen and Doug Hellinger (1999), *Coordinating Debt Relief on Adjustment – Creating the Conditions for More Indebtedness*, Washington D.C.: The Development GAP.

Haq, Israrul (15 April 2000), 'The Real Face of Clinton Doctrine', *Dawn – Internet Edition*, [http:// www. dawn. com].

Haq, Mahbub ul (1997), *Human Development in South Asia 1997*, Karachi: Oxford University Press.

Haq, Mahbub ul (1998), *Human Development in South Asia 1998*, Karachi: Oxford University Press.

Haq, Mahbub ul (1999), *Reflections on Human Development*, Karachi: Oxford University Press.

Harbor, Bernard & Chris Smith (1988), *The Arms Trade*, Hove: Wayland Publishers Ltd.

Hart, Henry H., 'Da Gama, Vasco', in Lauren S. Bahr (Editorial Director) (1995), *Collier's Encyclopaedia*, Vol. 7, New York: Collier's.

Hepworth, Mark (1989), *Geography of Information Economy*, London: Belhaven Press.

Hettne, Bjorn (1990), *The Development Theory and the Three Worlds,* New York: Longman.

Hobsbawn, Eric and Antonio Polito (1999), *The New Country*, London: Little Brown and Company.

Hoogvelt, A. (1982) *The Third World in Global Development,* London: Macmillan Press.

Hopwood, Derek (1998), The Culture of Modernity in Islam and the Middle East, in John Cooper, Ronald L. Nettler and Mohamed Mahmud (eds.), *Islam and Modernity*, London: I.B. Tauris.

Hornblower, Margot (6 December 1999), 'The Battle in Seattle – Anti-globalisation Forces are Threatening to Turn the WTO's meeting on Free Trade into a Free-for-All', *Time* (The Weekly).

Human Rights Watch – Asia (1996), *India – India's Secret Army in Kashmir – New Patterns of Abuse Emerge in the Conflict*, New York: Human Rights Watch – Asia.

Human Rights Watch (1991), *Human Rights in India – Kashmir Under Siege*, New York: Human Rights Watch.

Hunter, Jane (1999), *Israeli Foreign Policy – South Africa and Central America*, Boston: Southend Press.

Husain, Mir Zohair (1995), *Global Islamic Politic*, New York: Harper Collins College Publishers.

Hussain, Mushahid (11 February 1996) 'Central Asia's Quest for Security, *Nation* (The Daily), 11 February 1996.

Impact International (September 2000), Vol. 30-9.

Indonesia, Embassy of, (London) (unpublished).

International Institute for Strategic Studies (1999), *Military Balance 1999-2000*, London: Oxford University Press.

International Monitory Fund (May 1997), *World Economic Out Look - Globalization: Opportunities and Challenges,* Washington DC: IMF Publication Services.

Iqbal, Muhammad (1974), *The Reconstruction of Religious Thought in Islam*, New Delhi: Kitab Publishing House.

Irving, Thomas Ballentine, Khurshid Ahmad and Muhammad Manazir Ahsan (1979), *The Qur'ān: Basic Teachings*, Leicester: The Islamic Foundation.

Islamic Council of Europe (1979), *The Muslim World and the Future Economic Order*, London: Islamic Council of Europe.

Islamic Research and Training Institute (1992), *A Study of the Economic Cooperation Organisation with Special Reference to its Institutional Framework and Trade Promotion*, Jeddah: Islamic Research and Training Institute.

Jalebi, Jamil Ahmad (1953), *A History of Education in India*, Madras: J.S. & Co.

James Graff (26 June 2000), 'The Warm Embrace', *Time* (The Weekly).

Jan, Tark (1991), *Kashmir Suffers – A Sordid Tale Told by Western and Indian Journalists*, Islamabad: Institute of Policy Studies.

Jansen, G.H. (1980), *Militant Islam*, London: Pan Books, Ltd.

John Cloud (25 October 1999), 'Is It Trick or Treaty? The Critics have blasted the Senate for Rejecting a Nuclear Test-ban Treaty', *Time* (The Weekly).

Jubilee 2000 (July 2000) [http. www. Jublee2000uk.org].

Kahn, Jeremy (24 July 2000), 'The World's Largest Corporations', *The Fortnightly Fortune*, Vol. 142-3.

Kamal, Nazir (1996), *Denial of Freedom and Human Rights – A Review of Indian Repression in Kashmir*, Islamabad: The Institute of Strategic Studies.

Kamran, S. M. (1996), *South Asia- Convergence and Divergence*, Karachi: Idara-i-Adab.

Kelly, Majorie (ed) (1984), *Islam: The Religious and Political Life of a World Community*, New York: Praeger.

Khalid, M. Imran (1995), *History of Asian Subcontinent*, Karachi: Chashma Press.

Khaliq, S.A. (1973), *Pakistan – Peace and War*, London: Regency Press.

Khan, Inamullah, foreword in *History of Arakan*, published by the World Muslim Congress, p. iii, cited in Abdus Samad (1994), *Iqbal's Philosophy of Movement and Change*, Niigata-Ken, International University of Japan.

Khan, M. Fahim (1995), *Essays in Islamic Economics*, Leicester: The Islamic Foundation.

Khan, Nazir Ahmad (1978), *Commonwealth of Muslim States*, Lahore: Al-Ahibba.

Khan, Salahuddin Kasem (1996), 'Towards an Islamic Common Market: A Progressive Approach,' in Ayubur Rahman Bhuyan, *et. al.* (eds.), *Towards an Islamic Common Market: Proceedings of the International*

Seminar on Islamic Common Market held during December 18-20, 1993, Dhaka: Islamic Economic Research Bureau.

Khan, Waqar Masood (1985), *Towards an Interest-Free Islamic System*, Leicester: The Islamic Foundation.

Kharl, J.Y. (1997), *Back to the Past*, Lahore: Nashr-u-Ashait.

Kirn, Walter (24 April, 2000), in 'The New Radicals', *Time* (The Weekly).

Klasra, Rauf (23 April 2000), *Dawn – Internet Edition*, [http:// www. dawn.com].

Koreshi, S.M. (1995), *Western Fundamentalism in Action – New World Order*, Islamabad: Institute of Policy Studies.

Kosugi, Yasushi (1991), 'Restructuring Islamic Political Theories: Basic Concepts in a Contemporary Framework,' in Toshio Kuroda and Richard I. Lawless (eds.), *Nature of the Islamic Community*, Tokyo: Keiso Shobo Publishing Co.

Kupochan, Charles A. 1998), 'Defence Spending and Economic Performance', cited in Muhammad Siddique Alam, *Defence and Strategic Issues*, Karachi: Al-Hilal.

Laitin, David D. and Said S. Samatar (1987), *Somalia – Nation in Search of a State*, Boulder: Westview Press.

Lamb, Alastair (1991), *Kashmir – A Disputed Legacy, 1846-1990*, Hertingfordbury: Roxford Books.

Lamb, Alastair (1994), *Birth of A Tragedy – Kashmir 1947*, Hertingfordbury: Roxford Books.

Lamb, Alastair (1997), *Incomplete Partition – The Genesis of the Kashmir Dispute, 1947-1948*, Hertingfordbury: Roxford Books.

Landau, Jacob M. (1974), *The Politics of Pan-Islamism- Ideology and Organisation*, Oxford: Clarendon Press.

Lash, S. and J. Urry (1979), *The End of Organised Capitalism*, Oxford: Oxford University Press.

Latouche, Serge (1996), *The Westernisation of the World*, Cambridge: Polity Press.

Lipietz, A. (1987), *Miracles and Mirages: The Crisis of Global Fordism*, London: Verso.

Luckmann, Thomas (1967), *The Invisible Religion: The Problem Religion in a Modern Society,* New York: Macmillan.

Maddison, Angus (1999), 'Monitoring the World Economy', 1820-1992, Paris: Organisation for Economic Cooperation and Development, 1995, cited in UNDP, *Human Development Report 1999,* New York: Oxford University Press.

Madeley, John *et. al.* (1991), *When Aid is No Help: How Projects Fail, and How They Could Succeed,* London: Intermediate Technology Publications.

Madeley, John, Dee Sullivan and Jessica Woodroffe (1994), *Who Runs the World? (written for Christian Aid),* London: Christian Aid.

Magdoff, Harry (1992), *Monthly Review,* New York: Monthly Review Press.

Mahdi, Masud (24 June 2000), 'If ECO is to Forge Ahead', *Dawn - Internet Edition* [http://www.dawn.com].

Mannan, M.A (1989), *Economic Development and Social Peace in Islam,* London: Ta-Ha Publishers Ltd.

Mansfield, Peter (1976), *The Arabs,* London: Penguin Books.

Martin, Hans-Peter and Harald Schumann (Patrick Camiller [trans.]) (1997), *The Global Trap: Globalization & the Assault on Democracy & Prosperity,* London: Zed Book Ltd.

Masuel, Karmal (1999), *Disintegrating Global Economic Boundaries,* New Delhi: Digoo Press.

Mawdudi, Sayyid Abu A'la (1998), *Towards Understanding Islam,* Birmingham: Dawah Centre.

Mazuri, Ali, 'Islamic and Western Values', *Foreign Affairs,* September-October 1997.

McGreal, Ian P. (ed) (1995), *Great Thinkers of the Eastern World,* New York: Harper Collins Publishers.

Mckinnon, Michael and Peter Vine (1991), *Tides of War,* London: Boxtree Limited.

McLuhan, Marshal (1964), *Understanding Media: The Extension of Man,* New York: McGraw-Hill Book Company.

Miller, Judith (19 September 2000), 'U.S. Asks Putin Not to Sell Iran a Laser System', *New York Times* (The Daily).

Miller, Judith (20 October 1999), 'US Once Deployed 12,000 Atom Arms in Two Dozen Nations', *New York Times*.

Mirza, Shiraz Akhtar (2000), *National and International Affairs*, Karachi: Samee and Sons.

Mittelman, James H. (1997) *'Globalization: Critical Reflections'*, Boulder: Lynne Rienner Publishers Inc.

Mohammadi, Ali (1997), *International Communication and Globalisation*, London: Sage.

Morgenthau, Hans J., Kenneth W. Thompson (1991), *Politics Among Nations: The Struggle for Power and Peace,* Lahore: Vanguard Books Pvt. Ltd.

Najam, A. (1981), 'Islam and Arab Nationalism,' in Michael Curtis (ed), *Religion and the Politics in the Middle East,* Colorado: Westview Press.

Naqvi, Syed Nawab Haider, *et. al.* (1984), *Principles of Islamic Economic Reforms*, Islamabad: Pakistan Institute of Development Economics.

Naqvi, Syed Nawab Haider, *et. al.* (1989), *An Agenda for Islamic Economic Reforms*, Islamabad: Pakistan Institute of Development Economics.

Nasr, Seyyed Hossein (1994), *Traditional Islam in the Modern World*, London: Kegan Paul International.

Nasr, Seyyed Vali Reza (1995), 'Muhammad Iqbal', in Ian P. McGreal (ed.) (1995), *Great Thinkers of the Eastern World*, New York: Harper Collins Publishers.

National Scientific Committee – Sudan, *A Report on Al-Shifa Factory* (unpublished), London: Embassy of Sudan, London.

New International Publications Ltd. (1999), *The World Guide 1999/2000*, Oxford: New International Publications Ltd.

New Internationalist (issues: May and August 2000) (The Monthly).

New Internationalist Publications Ltd. (2000), *The World Guide*, Oxford: New Internationalist Publications Ltd.

New York Times (various issues).

Newburg, Pamela (9-15 June 1994), 'Indo-Pakistan Relations: Old Diplomacy Must be laid to Rest', *The Friday Times* (The Weekly).

Norris, Robert S., William M. Arkin and William Burr (November-December 1999), 'Where They Were', *Bulletin of the Atomic Scientists*, Vol. 55-6.

Nurullah, Syed and J.P. Naik (1951), *A History of Education in India*, Bombay: Macmillan & Co. Ltd.

O'Brien, Patrick K. (ed.) (1999), *Atlas of World History – From the Origin of the Humanity to the Year 2000*, London: Institute of Historical Research.

Offe, K. (1985), *Disorganized Capitalism*, Oxford: Polity Press.

Ovendale, Ritchie (1999), *The Origins of The Arab-Israeli Wars*, London: Longman.

Oxfam (1995), *A Case for Reform – Fifty Years of the IMF and the World Bank*, Oxford: Oxfam.

Pakistan, Embassy of, (London) (unpublished).

Pakistan, Government of, (n.d.), *Kashmir in the Security Council*, Islamabad.

Parliamentary Human Rights Group (1991), *Human Rights Abuses in Kuwait*, London: Parliamentary Human Rights Group.

Parsons, Talcott (1966), 'Religion in a Modern Pluralistic Society', *Review of Religious Research*, Vol. 7.

Pasha, Mustapha Kamal, and Ahmed I. Samatar (1997), 'The Resurgence of Islam', in James H. Mittelman (ed) (1997), *Globalization: Critical Reflections*, Boulder: Lynne Reinner Publishers Inc.

Paul, Pope John (2 May 2000), *Dawn, Internet Edition* [http:// www. dawn.com].

Payer, Cheryl (1991), *Lent and Lost: Foreign Credit and Third World Development*, Atlantic Highlands: Zed Books.

Perlez, Jane (29 November 1999), 'U.S. Weighs Using Food as Support for Sudan Rebels', *New York Times* (The Daily).

Peterson, Scott (2000), *Me Against My Brother – At War in Somalia, Sudan, and Rwanda*, New York: Routledge.

Pilger, John, 'Collateral Damage', in Anthony Arnove, *Iraq Under Siege – The Deadly Impact of Sanctions and War*, London: Pluto Press, 2000, quoted from Leslie Stahl (12 May 12, 1996), 'Punishing Saddam', produced by Catherine Olian, CBS, *60 Minutes*.

Presse, Agence France (1998), quoted in Sean Gabb, *Why has Britain Supported American State Terrorism Against Sudan? Where is the Evidence? – An Open Letter to the British Prime Minister, Rt. Hon. Tony Blair MP*, London: The Sudan Foundation.

Preston, P.W. (1996), *Development Theory: An Introduction*, Oxford: Blackwell Publishers Ltd.

Proctor, Harris (ed) (1969), *Islam and International Relations*, London: Full Hebb Press.

Rafai, Syed Noorul Hassan and Abdul Kabeer Karipak (eds.) (1990), *Kashmir Bleeds (Prepared by the Human Rights Commission Srinagar)*, Islamabad: Institute of Policy Studies.

Rahnema, Majid and Victoria Bawtree (eds) (1997), *The Post-Development Reader*, London: Zed Books Ltd., 1997.

Rashid, Ahmad (1994) *The Resurgence of Central Asia: Islam or Nationalism?* Karachi: Oxford University Press, 1994.

Rehman, Khalid, *et. al.* (1999), *Jama'at-e-Islami and National and International Politics* (Vol. II), Lahore: Shirkat Printing Press.

Rehman, S.M. (ed.) (1998), *Central Asia – Regional Cooperation for Peace and Development*, Rawalpindi: Foundation for Research on International Environment National Development and Security.

Reuters (26 August 1998 at 6:43 AM EDT) 'US State Department says Soil Showed VX-Sudan Link', cited in Sean Gabb (ed.), *American Claims About the Al-Shifa Factory Put to the Test*, London: The Sudan Foundation, 1998.

Rich, Bruce (1994), *Mortgaging the Earth: The World Bank, Environmental Impoverishment and the Crisis of Development*, London: Earthscan Publications Ltd.

Riddell, Roger (1996), *Aid in the 21st Century*, New York: UNDP.

Risen, James, 'Question of Evidence: A Special Report', *The New York Times*, 27 October 1999.

Robertson, Ronald (1987), 'Globalization and Socital Modernization: A note on Japan and Japanese Religion', *Sociological Analysis,* Vol. 47 (S).

Robertson, Ronald (1992), *Globalisation,* London: Sage.

Sachs, Jeffery (24 June 2000), 'Sachs on Globalisation: A New Map of the World', *Economist* (The Weekly).

Saeed, Khawaja Amjad (1999), *Economy of Pakistan,* Lahore: Institute of Business Management.

Safieh, Afif (1999), *Children of a Lesser God?,* London: Palestinian General Delegation to the UK and the Office of Representation of the PLO to the Holy See.

Said, Edward (4 March 2000), Reflections on US Injustice, *Dawn – Internet Edition* [http://www.dawn.com].

Said, Edward W. (1997), *Covering Islam: How the Media and the Experts Determine - How we See the Rest of the World,* London: Vintage.

Saif, Abu (25 June 2000), 'Crippling Effects of Sanctions', *Dawn – Internet Edition* [http://www.dawn.com].

Salahddeen, Mohamed, (19 August 1997) The Plight of Kashmir', *Al-Madinah.*

Salam, Abdus (July 1983), 'Science in the Islamic World', *Higher Education Review: A Quarterly Journal of the University Grant Commission, Pakistan,* Vol. 1-3.

Samad, Abdus (1992), *Iqbal's Concept of State,* Niigata-Ken: International University of Japan.

Samad, Abdus (1994), *Iqbal's Philosophy of Movement and Change,* Niigata-Ken, International University of Japan.

Sarwar, Ghulam (1994), *Islam – Belief and Teachings,* London: Muslim Educational Trust.

Sarwar, Ghulam (1997), *OIC – Contemporary Issues of the Muslim World,* Rawalpindi: Foundation for Research on International Environment National Development and Security.

Sarwar, Ghulam (February 1997), 'Governance and Dispensation of Justice in Pakistan,' *National Development and Security: Quarterly Journal,* Vol. V-3.

Sasson, Jeans P. (1991), *The Rape of Kuwait – The True Story of Iraqi Atrocities Against a Civilian Population,* New York: Knightsbridge Publishing Company.

178

Saudi Arabia, Embassy of, (Washington) (1989), *Understanding Islam and Muslims*, Cambridge: Islamic Text Society.

Sayeed, M.J. (31 May 2000), 'Indian Atrocities', *Dawn – Internet Edition* [http://www.dawn.com].

Schaeffer, Robert (1999), *Warpath – the Politics of Partition*, New York: Hill & Wang.

Schenker, Jennifer L. (11 October 1999), 'New Technology Could Help Narrow the Information Gap Between the Developed and the Developing Worlds', *Time* (The Weekly).

Shaikh, Abdul Rauf (1987), *The Vision – The Selections From the Holy Qur'ān*, Rawalpindi: Hafeez Printing Corporation.

Shakweer, Farooq (1996), 'Prospects for the Establishment of the Islamic Common Market and the Role of the Islamic Development Bank', in Ayubur Rahman Bhuyan, *et. al.* (eds), *Towards an Islamic Common Market, Proceedings of the International Seminar on Islamic Common Market held During December 18-20, 1993*, Dhaka: Islamic Economic Research Bureau.

Shalaby, Ismail (January-March 1988), 'The Islamic Common Market', *Journal of Islamic Banking and Finance*.

Sharp, H. (ed) (1922), *Selections from Educational Records: Part-II*, Calcutta, Government Printing Press.

Sibtain, Tahira (1993), *Kashmir and the United Nations*, Islamabad: National Institute of Pakistan Studie.

Siddiqi, Muhammad Nejatullah (1979), 'Banking in an Islamic Framework', in Salem Azzam, *The Muslim World and the Future Economic Order*, London: Islamic Council of Europe.

Siddiqi, Muhammad Nejatullah (1983), *Issues in Islamic Banking: Selected Papers*, Leicester: The Islamic Foundation.

Siddiqi, Muhammad Nejatullah (1985), *Insurance in an Islamic Economy*, Leicester: Islamic Foundation.

Siddiqi, Muhammad Nejatullah (1988), *Banking Without Interest*, Leicester: The Islamic Foundation.

Siddiqi, Muhammad Nejatullah (1996), *Role of the State in the Economy – An Islamic Perspective*, Leicester: The Islamic Foundation.

Smith, Charles D. (1996), *Palestine and the Arab-Israeli Conflict*, New York: St. Martin's Press.

Sontag, Deborah (25 November 1999), 'Israel Eases Security Over Nuclear Whistle-Blower's Trial', *New York Times*.

Sudan Foundation (October 2000), *Politics Files* (various issues) [http://www.sufo.demon.co.uk].

Sunkel, O. (1977), 'The Development of Development Thinking', *IDS Bulletin*, XXXI-3.

Supple, Carrie (1993), *From Prejudice to Genocide – Learning About the Holocaust*, Stoke-on-Trent: Trentham Books Ltd.

Syed, Fasahat H. (1997), 'A Pragmatic Approach to Ensure Progress of the Muslim World,' in Ghulam Sarwar (ed), *OIC: Contemporary Issues of the Muslim World*, Rawalpindi: Foundation for Research on International environment National Development and Security.

Tabibi, Abdul Hakim (March 1997), 'Islamic Solidarity', *Islamic Order*.

Tash, Abdul Qader, (Editor-in-Chief, Arab News) (22 June 1997), ' The West's Clouded View of Arabs and Islam, *Arab News*, [http:// www. arab.net/ arabview/ articles/ tash27. html].

Tellis, Kenneth T. (10 April 2000) 'Clinton's Double Standard', *Dawn – Internet Edition*, [http://www.dawn.com].

Thirlwall, A.P. (1992), *Growth and Development - with Special Reference to Developing Economies*, London: Macmillan.

Thomas, Alan and Ben Crow *et. al* (1997), *Third World Atlas – Second Edition*, Buckingham: Open University Press.

Time (various issues) (The Weekly).

Todaro, Michael P. (1989), *Economic Development in the Third World*, London: Longman.

U.S. Department of State, 'International Information Programme' (21 August 2000), *Fact Sheet: World Military Expenditures and Arms Transfer 1998* [http:// www. usinfo. state.gov/ topical/ pol/arms/stories/ 00082101.htm].

Uddin, Mughees (May 1995), 'Role of Uncontrolled Media in a Controlled Society: The Case Study of Iranian Revolution', *National Development and Security: A Quarterly Journal*, Vol. III-4.

180

UNCTAD (26 January 2000), *Trade and Development Report 1999* [http://www.unctad.org].

UNDP (1990), *Human Development Report 1990*, New York: Oxford University Press.

UNDP (1994), *Human Development Report 1994*, New York: Oxford University Press.

UNDP (1998), *Human Development Report 1998*, New York: Oxford University Press.

UNDP (1999), *Human Development Report 1999*, New York: Oxford University Press.

UNDP (2000), *Human Development Report 2000*, New York: Oxford University Press.

UNESCO (1998), *World Education Report 1998*, Paris: UNESCO Publishing.

UNICEF (1997), *The State of the World's Children 1998*, New York: Oxford University Press.

United Nations (1998), *World Economic and Social Survey 1998: Trends and Policies in the World Economy*, New York: United Nations.

United States Information Services (28 September 2000), [http:// www. usinfo.state.gov/ regional/ea/timor].

UNO, Conciliation Commission for Palestine, *Report of the United Nations Economic Survey Mission*, New York: United Nations Document A/AC.25/6, cited in *CAABU*, No. 4 (Council for the Advancement of Arab-British Understanding, London).

US Department of State, Bureau of Democracy (February 2000), *Human Rights and Labor, Burma: 1999 Country Report on Human Rights Practices* [http:// www. usinfo. state.gov/ global].

Vindal, John (5 December 1999), 'Real Battle For Seattle', *Observer* (The Daily).

Waters, Malcolm (1995), *Globalization*, London: Routledge.

Watkins, Kevin (1995), *The Oxfam Poverty Report*, Oxford: Oxfam.

Watt, W. Montgomery (1980), *Islamic Political Thought*, New York: Columbia University Press.

Weiner, Myron, (1974), 'Political Integration and Political Development' in Frank Tachau *The Developing Nations: What Path to Modernization?* New York: Dodd, Mead & Company.

Williams, John Alden (ed.) (1971), *Themes of Islamic Civilisation*, California: University of California Press.

World Bank (2000), The, *World Development Indicators*, Washington, D.C.: The World Bank.

World Bank, (1999), *World Development Report 1999-2000: Entering in the 21st Century*, New York: Oxford University Press.

World Bank, The (1990), *World Development Report 1990*, New York: Oxford University Press.

World Bank, The (1992), *Effective Implementation: Key to Development Impact*, Washington, D.C.: The World Bank.

World Kashmir Freedom Movement (unpublished).

Yahya Effendi (November 1999), 'South Asia in the Nuclear Trap', *National Development and Security*, Vol. VIII-2.

Zakzouk, Mahmoud (1996), 'Peace from an Islamic Standpoint: World Peace as a Concept and Necessity,' in Andreas Beteh (ed.), *Peace for Humanity – Principles, Problems and Perspectives of the Future as Seen by Muslims and Christians*, New Delhi: Vikas Publishing House Ltd.

Zaman, S.M. Hasanuz (1991), *Economic Function of an Islamic State*, Leicester: The Islamic Foundation.

Appendix

Basic Data – Muslim and the Non-Muslim Worlds

Country	Popu-lation (million) 1998	Surface Area (000 sq. km).	GNP US$, 1998 (1990s) Total (billion)	GNP US$, 1998 (1990s) Per capita	Population blow poverty line	GDP growth rate 1985-98
Muslim World						
Afghanistan	26 (99)	652	2.7	164	..	..
Albania	3 (70)	29	2.7	810	19.6 (1996)	-1.3
Algeria	30 (99)	2,382	46.5	1,550	22.6 (1995)	0.1
Azerbaijan	8 (93)	87	3.9	490	..	-11.8
Bahrain	0.6 (100)	1	4.9	7,660	..	-1.4
Bangladesh	126 (87)	144	44.0	350	35.6 (1995-96)	2.2
Benin	6 (15)	113	2.3	380	33.0 (1989-94)	0.7
Brunei	0.3 (63)	6	9.0	30,000	..	-1.0
Burkina Faso	11 (25)	274	2.6	240	..	1.2
Cameroon	14 (16)	475	8.7	610	..	0.1
Chad	7 (45)	1,284	1.7	230	..	0.3
Comoros	0.5 (86)	2	0.2	370	..	-1.1
Djibouti	0.6 (94)	23	0.5	960	..	..
Egypt	61 (96)	1,001	79.2	1,290	..	3.6
Gabon	1 (..)	268	4.6	3,950	..	-1.6
Gambia	1 (96)	11	0.4	340	64.0 (1989-94)	-0.1
Guinea	7 (85)	247	3.8	450	..	1.4

Country	Population (million) 1998	Surface Area (000 sq. km).	GNP US$, 1998 (1990s)		Population blow poverty line	GDP growth rate 1985-98
			Total (billion)	Per capita		
Guinea Bissau	1 (90)	36	0.2	160	49.0 (1989-94)	0.3
Indonesia	204 (90)	1,905	138.5	680	15.1 (1990)	5.1
Iran	62 (99)	1,633	109.6	1,770	..	-1.6
Iraq	22 (98)	438	20.0	1,036	..	-11.2
Jordan	5 (92)	89	6.9	1,520	15.0 (1989-94)	2.3
Kazakhstan	16 (47)	2,717	20.6	1,310	65.0 (1989-95)	-6.6
Kuwait	2 (85)	18	32.8	16,400	..	-1.5
Kyrgyzstan	5 (75)	199	1.6	350	88.0 (1989-95)	9.4
Lebanon	4 (57)	10	15.0	3,560	..	..
Libya	5 (97)	1760	23.3	4,755	..	-4.5
Malaysia	22 (53)	330	79.8	3,600	16.0 (1989-94)	4.6
Maldives	0.3 (100)	0.3	0.3	1,230	..	5.4
Mali	11 (90)	1,240	2.6	250	..	0.6
Mauritania	3 (100)	1,026	1.0	410	57.0 (1989-94)	0.0
Morocco	28 (99)	447	34.8	1,250	..	1.7
Niger	10 (80)	1,267	1.9	190	13.1 (1990-91)	-1.7
Nigeria	121 (70)	924	36.4	300	34.1 (1992-93)	-0.5
Oman	2 (98)	213	10.3	6,440	..	2.1
Pakistan	132 (96)	796	63.2	480	34.0 (1989-94)	2.9
Palestine	3 (75)	6	..	..	..	..
Qatar	0.7 (95)	11	7.0	14,000	..	..
Saudi Arabia	21 (100)	2,150	105.0	6.610	..	-2.6
Senegal	9 (92)	197	4.8	530	..	-0.3

Muslim World						
Country	Population (million) 1998	Surface Area (000 sq. km).	GNP US$, 1998 (1990s)		Population blow poverty line	GDP growth rate 1985-98
			Total (billion)	Per capita		
Sierra Leone	5 (70)	72	0.7	140	75.0 (1989-94)	-2.2
Somalia	10 (100)	638	0.8	80	..	..
Sudan	28 (75)	2,506	7.2	269	..	-0.9
Syria	15 (92)	185	15.6	1,020	..	1.2
Tajikistan	6 (95)	143	2.1	350	..	-11.2
Tunisia	9 (98)	164	19.2	210	14.1 (1990)	2.5
Turkey	63 (99)	775	200.0	3,160	..	2.0
Turkmenistan	5 (85)	448	6.4	1,650	61.0 (1989-95)	..
U.A.E	3 (96)	84	48.7	18,220	..	-2.9
Uganda	21 (25)	241	6.7	320	55.0 (1989-94)	1.9
Uzbekistan	24 (88)	447	20.9	870	63.0 (1989-95)	..
Yemen	16 (97)	528	4.9	300	..	..
Non-Muslim World						
Country	Population (million) 1998	Surface Area (000 sq. km).	GNP US$, 1998 (1990s)		Population blow poverty line	GDP growth rate 1985-98
			Total (billion)	Per capita		
Angola	12	1,247	4.1	340	..	-1.9
Antigua & Barbuda	0.1	0.4	0.6	8,300	12.0 (1989-94)	5.0
Argentina	36	2,780	324.1	8,970	26.0 (1989-94)	0.3
Armenia	4	30	1.8	480	..	-3.3
Australia	19	7,741	380.6	20,300	7.8 (1989-95)	1.7
Austria	8	84	217.2	26,850	8.0 (1989-95)	2.1
Bahamas	0.3	14	3	10,000	..	2.2

Non-Muslim World					
Country	Popu-lation (million) 1998	Surface Area (000 sq. km).	GNP US$, 1998 (1990s)		Population blow poverty line	GDP growth rate 1985-98
			Total (billion)	Per capita		
Barbados	0.3	0.4	2.1	7,890	..	1.3
Belarus	10	208	22.5	2,200	22.0 (1989-95)	-2.0
Belgium	10	33	259.0	25,380	12.0 (1989-95)	1.8
Belize	0.2	23	0.6	2,610	35.0 (1989-94)	2.3
Bhutan	0.8	47	0.3	163	..	4.1
Bolivia	8	1,099	7.9	1,000	..	-0.1
Bosnia & Herzegovina	5 (45)	51	4.0	800	..	..
Botswana	2	582	5.6	3,600	..	5.7
Brazil	166	8,547	758.0	4,570	17.0 (1989-94)	1.1
Bulgaria	8 (13)	111	10.1	1,230	15.0 (1989-95)	0.0
Burundi	7 (1)	28	0.9	140	..	-0.5
Cambodia	11 (2)	181	3.0	280	36.1 (1997)	2.9
Canada	31	9,971	612.2	20,020	5.9 (1989-95)	1.5
Cape Verde	0.5	4	0.4	1,060	44.0 (1989-94)	2.8
Cen. African Republic	3 (10)	623	1.0	300	..	0.6
Chile	15	757	71.3	4,810	20.5 (1994)	3.9
China	1,246 (3)	9,598	10872	750	6.0 (1996)	7.8
Colombia	41	1,139	106.8	2,600	17.7 (1992)	2.0
Congo (Republic)	3	342	1.9	690	..	0.6
Congo (Demo. Rep.)	48 (10)	2,345	5.3	110	..	-5.1
Costa Rica	4	51	9.8	2,780	11.0 (1989-94)	0.7
Côte d'Ivoire	14 (30)	322	10.1	700	..	-1.2
Croatia	5 (1)	57	20.7	4,520	..	..

Non-Muslim World					
Country	Popu-lation (million) 1998	Surface Area (000 sq. km).	GNP US$, 1998 (1990s)		Population blow poverty line	GDP growth rate 1985-98
			Total (billion)	Per capita		
Cuba	11	111	20.9	1,935	..	..
Cyprus	0.8 (18)	9	6.1	8,615	..	6.2
Czech Republic	10	79	51.8	5,040	1.0 (1989-95)	-0.2
Denmark	5	43	176.4	33,260	7.6 (1989-95)	2.0
Dominica	0.1	1	0.2	3,010	33.0 (1989-94)	3.4
Dominican Republic	8	49	14.6	1,770	20.6 (1992)	1.6
Ecuador	12	284	18.6	1,530	35.0 (1989-94)	0.9
El Salvador	6	21	11.2	1,850	38.0 (1989-94)	-0.3
Equatorial Guinea	0.5	28	0.6	1,500	..	8.0
Eritrea	4 (45)	118	0.8	200	..	..
Estonia	1	45	4.9	3,390	37.0 (1989-95)	-0.7
Ethiopia	61 (45)	1,104	6.1	100	..	-0.4
Fiji	0.8 (8)	18	1.7	2,110	..	0.9
Finland	5	338	124.3	24,110	3.8 (1989-95)	1.8
France	59 (2)	552	1,466.2	24,940	12.0 (1989-95)	1.7
Georgia	5 (11)	70	5.1	930	..	..
Germany	82 (2)	357	2,122.7	25,850	11.5 (1989-95)	..
Ghana	18 (30)	239	7.2	390	31.0 (1989-94)	-0.2
Greece	11 (1)	132	122.9	11,650	..	1.7
Grenada	0.1	0.3	0.3	3,170	20.0 (1989-94)	3.4
Guatemala	11	109	17.7	1,640	58.0 (1989-94)	0.4
Guyana	0.9 (9)	215	0.7	770	43.0 (1989-94)	-0.7

Country	Population (million) 1998	Surface Area (000 sq. km).	GNP US$, 1998 (1990s)		Population blow poverty line	GDP growth rate 1985-98
			Total (billion)	Per capita		
Haiti	8	28	3.1	410	..	-1.4
Honduras	6	112	4.5	730	53.0 (1989-94)	0.7
Hungary	10	93	45.6	4,510	4.0 (1989-95)	1.4
Iceland	0.3	103	7.7	28,010	..	2.3
India	980 (14)	3,288	421.3	430	35.0 (1994)	3.0
Ireland	4	70	67.5	18,340	36.5 (1989-95)	4.0
Israel	6 (15)	21	95.2	15,940	..	2.0
Italy	58	301	1,166.2	20,250	2.0 (1989-95)	2.2
Jamaica	3	11	4.3	1,680	32.0 (1989-94)	-0.5
Japan	126	378	4,089.9	32,380	3.7 (1989-95)	2.8
Kenya	29 (30)	580	9.7	330	37.0 (1989-94)	0.5
Korea, DR (North)	23	121	..	..	..	..
Korea, Rep. (South)	46	99	369.9	7,970	..	6.8
Lao PDR	5 (1)	237	1.6	330	46.0 (1989-94)	2.9
Latvia	2	65	5.9	2,430	22.0 (1989-95)	-0.3
Lesotho	2	30	1.2	570	26.0 (1989-95)	3.8
Liberia	3 (20)	111	1.2	430	..	..
Lithuania	4	65	9.0	2,440	30.0 (1989-95)	-2.1
Luxembourg	0.4	3	18.6	43,570	4.3 (1989-95)	3.4
Macedonia	2	26	2.6	1,290	..	..
Madagascar	15 (7)	587	3.8	260	59.0 (1989-94)	-2.0
Malawi	11 (20)	118	2.1	200	..	0.3
Malta	0.4	0.3	3.6	9,440	..	5.5

Table heading: **Non-Muslim World**

			Non-Muslim World			
Country	Popu-lation (million) 1998	Surface Area (000 sq. km).	GNP US$, 1998 (1990s)		Population blow poverty line	GDP growth rate 1985-98
			Total (billion)	Per capita		
Martinique	0.4	1	..	..	..	..
Mauritius	1 (17)	2	4.2	3,700	11.0 (1989-94)	4.3
Mexico	96	1,958	380.9	3,970	34.0 (1989-94)	0.9
Moldova	4	34	1.8	410	66.0 (1989-95)	..
Mongolia	3	1,567	1.0	440	36.0 (1989-94)	..
Mozambique	17 (20)	802	3.6	210	..	1.1
Myanmar	44 (5)	677	37.7	863	..	..
Namibia	2	824	3.2	1,940	..	-0.7
Nepal	23 (3)	147	4.8	210	..	1.7
Netherlands	16 (3)	41	388.7	24,760	14.4 (1989-95)	1.7
New Zealand	4	271	55.8	14,700	..	0.8
Nicaragua	5	130	1.4	350	50.0 (1989-94)	-2.9
Norway	4	324	152.1	34,330	2.6 (1989-95)	3.0
Panama	3	76	8.5	3,080	..	0.8
Papua New Guinea	5	463	4.1	890	..	0.5
Paraguay	5	407	9.2	1,760	22.0 (1989-94)	1.6
Peru	25	1,285	61.1	2,460	49.0 (1997)	-0.3
Philippines	75 (5)	300	78.9	1,050	37.5 (1997)	0.6
Poland	39	323	150.8	3,900	20.0 (1989-95)	0.8
Portugal	10	92	106.4	10,690	..	2.7
Puerto Rico	4	9	..	..	..	..
Romania	22 (2)	238	31.3	1,390	59.0 (1989-95)	1.3
Russian Federation	147	18,075	337.9	2,300	50.0 (1989-95)	0.9

			Non-Muslim World			

Country	Population (million) 1998	Surface Area (000 sq. km).	GNP US$, 1998 (1990s)		Population blow poverty line	GDP growth rate 1985-98
			Total (billion)	Per capita		
Rwanda	8 (1)	26	1.9	230	53.0 (1989-94)	-0.5
Samoa (Western)	0.2	3	0.2	1,020	..	0.0
São Tomé & Principe	0.1	1	0.04	280	46.0 (1989-94)	-1.4
Seychelles	0.1	0.5	0.5	6,450	..	2.8
Singapore	3 (20)	1	95.1	30,060	..	5.7
Slovak Republic	5	49	20.0	3,700	1.0 (1989-95)	0.2
Slovenia	2 (1)	20	19.4	9,760	1.0 (1989-95)	..
Solomon Islands	0.4	29	0.3	650	..	3.2
South Africa	41 (3)	1,221	119.0	2,880	..	-0.6
Spain	39	506	553.7	14,080	21.1 (1989-95)	1.8
Sri Lanka	19 (8)	66	15.2	810	35.3 (1990-91)	3.2
Suriname	0.4 (2)	163	0.7	1,660	..	3.0
Swaziland	1	17	1.4	1,400	..	1.3
Sweden	9	450	226.9	25,620	4.6 (1989-95)	1.1
Switzerland	7	41	284.8	40,080	..	0.9
Tanzania	32 (31)	945	6.7	210	50.0 (1989-94)	..
Thailand	61 (4)	513	134.4	2,200	13.1 (1992)	5.7
Togo	4 (10)	57	1.5	330	17.3 (1989-94)	-0.8
Trinidad & Tobago	1 (9)	5	5.8	4,430	21.0 (1989-94)	0.2
Ukraine	50	604	42.7	850	63.0 (1989-95)	-8.3
United Kingdom	59 (3)	245	1,263.8	21,400	13.1 (1989-95)	1.9
United State	270 (4)	9,364	7,921.3	29,340	14.1 (1989-95)	1.6
Uruguay	3	177	20.3	6,180	..	1.5

Non-Muslim World						
Country	Popu-lation (million) 1998	Surface Area (000 sq. km).	GNP US$, 1998 (1990s)		Population blow poverty line	GDP growth rate 1985-98
			Total (billion)	Per capita		
Vanuatu	0.2	12	0.2	1,270	..	-0.7
Venezuela	23	912	81.3	3,500	31.0 (1989-94)	-0.8
Viet Nam	78	332	25.6	330	51.0 (1989-94)	..
Yugoslavia (Serb./Mont.)	11 (19)	102	13.5	1,298	..	..
Zambia	10 (24)	753	3.2	330	86.0 (1993)	-1.7
Zimbabwe	12 (1)	12	7.1	610	26.0 (1989-94)	0.0

Source:
- The World Bank (1999), *World Development Report 1999/2000*, New York: Oxford University Press, pp. 230-31, 236-37, 250-51, 272.
- Ian Castello-Cortes, *et. al.* (eds.) (editions: 1994, 1995, 1998, 1999), *World Reference Atlas*, London: Dorling Kindersley Ltd.
- New Internationalist Publications Ltd. (2000), *The World Guide*, Oxford: New Internationalist Publications Ltd., pp. 85-601.
- Naeem Dar (ed.) (1999), *Muslim Directory*, London: Blackmore Press, pp. 188-220.
- Ghulam Sarwar (1994), Islam – Belief and Teachings, London: Muslim Educational Trust, pp. 204-09.
- The Economist Intelligence Unit (various country reports), London.
- CIA (July 2000), *World Factbook 1999* [http://www. odci.gov/ cia/publications/ factbook].
- UNDP (1999), *Human Development Report 1999*, New York: Oxford University Press, pp. 146-50 (data refer to the most recent year during 1989-94).

Note:
- Figures in the parentheses (col. 2) are the percentage of Muslim population in respective countries.
- Every effort has been made to complete this table to the maximum extent. Thus various sources were used in this regard. In some cases figures of col. 2, 4 and 5 do not exactly match with each other because difference of sources.
- For some countries, figures in col. 5 and 5 are other than 1998 (nearest year) which due to the use of different sources, too.

Index

192